THE ILLUSION OF INTELLIGENCE

Why AI Feels Smart, Where It Goes Wrong, and What to Do About It

---

J. A. COLE

First published 2026

First edition

Published by Solo Systems Foundry

SoloSystemsFoundry.com

Paperback ISBN: 978-0-6487051-2-3

J. A. Cole

Melbourne, Australia

CONTENTS

CHAPTER 1

The Lie You've Been Using

"The expectation itself is where things went wrong."

AI, Artificial Intelligence, is exactly what AI is NOT.

You open a chat window because it feels like the faster option.

There is something you need to get done. A proposal you have written before. A LinkedIn post you have been meaning to finish. An email that has been sitting half-done for longer than it should. You type a few lines, press enter, and the response arrives almost instantly. Clean. Structured. It reads well enough that for a moment, the problem feels solved.

Then you slow down and actually read it.

At first, it holds together. The sentences make sense, the flow is there, and it looks like something you could send. Then something small starts to shift. A word you would not choose. A phrase that is slightly too smooth. The tone lands somewhere near yours, but not where you actually live.

You adjust it. A sentence gets rewritten, a word gets swapped. You ask again, trying to guide it a little closer. It responds, and it is better. Closer, but still not right. You keep what works and fix what does not. It takes longer than you expected, but you get there.

The next time, you try to get ahead of it. You explain more, give it more context, try to be clearer about what you want. The output improves, but the same pattern shows up. Almost right. Not quite yours. You fix it again.

So it becomes a rhythm. You are not starting from scratch, and you are not using what comes back as-is. You are somewhere in between, shaping something that was supposed to save you time into something that actually feels usable. Some days it genuinely does save time. Other days it drifts sideways into a different kind of work, less writing and more correcting.

The output is not failing. That is precisely what makes it hard to pin down. It is useful enough that you keep coming back, competent enough that you hesitate to dismiss it. It produces something every single time. It just does not produce something you fully trust without stepping in.

So you keep stepping in.

You rewrite parts of it, guide it again, try a different way of asking. You assume there is a better way to get what you want out of it, and that you have not quite found it yet. That the gap between what it gives you and what you need is something you can close with a better instruction, a clearer prompt, a slightly more refined approach.

And because it keeps getting close, there is always enough to justify trying once more. It feels like progress. But something is still off.

Close Enough to Keep You Coming Back

You keep using it because it does help.

There are moments where it gives you something clean enough that you barely touch it. A sentence that lands. A structure that holds. A starting point that saves you from the blank page. In those moments, it feels like it is doing exactly what you hoped it would.

Then the next time, it does not.

Same kind of task, same level of effort going in. The output comes back looking fine on the surface but needing work. More than you expected. You find yourself reading it carefully, line by line, checking it in a way you would not check something you had written yourself.

You do not fully trust it.

That trust never quite settles, even after months of using it. You adapt to the pattern instead. You learn that it will get you part of the way there, and that you will need to take it the rest of the way yourself. You stop expecting it to be right and start expecting to fix it. Some days that trade feels worth it. Other days it feels like you are doing a different version of the same work, just broken into two stages.

What makes it harder is that you can see what it is capable of. It is not random, not obviously broken. It can produce something that looks like it understands what you are trying to do, and that is what keeps the expectation alive: the sense that it should be able to do this properly, consistently, if you could just get it there.

So when it falls short, it does not feel like a limitation of the tool. It feels like something you have not figured out yet.

The Accumulation You've Stopped Noticing

The problem is rarely dramatic.

It is usually a sentence you change without thinking too much about it. A phrase that sounds slightly too polished. A paragraph that says roughly the right thing in a way you would never actually say it. Nothing broken enough to stop everything. Just small corrections, over and over.

You remove a word because it feels off, tighten a sentence because it drifts, ask for another version because the first sounded flat and then another because the second leaned too far the other way. You start reading every response with a low-level suspicion already in place, scanning for the part where it quietly stops sounding like you.

Sometimes it gives you something that looks finished until you slow down and notice it has missed the point slightly. Subtle enough to pass a quick read, but impossible to leave alone once you catch it.

Rachel knows this moment. She is a freelance copywriter in Bristol, four years into running the business on her own. Last week AI gave her three paragraphs for a client proposal: her approach, her process, what separates her work from the agency option. It came back structured and clean. She read it through and something started to shift. Every sentence sounded like it was written for a copywriter in her category rather than for her specifically. She spent twenty minutes removing phrases like "leveraging your unique methodology to drive meaningful outcomes" before giving up on the middle paragraph and rewriting it herself. The proposal got sent. The client was happy. Nobody would have known. But she knows exactly how that twenty minutes went, and she knows it will go the same way next time.

Rachel will appear throughout this book. Her days may look like yours.

Then there is the second-guessing.

You question what it wrote, then you question what you asked. Was the instruction too vague? Did you give it the wrong context? Should you have framed it differently? You do not just edit the answer. You start revising the conversation that produced the answer, as if the mistake might have begun one step earlier.

This is where the time goes. A hundred small interruptions, each one easy to dismiss, each one adding up. Tiny moments of friction that are easy to pass by because each one seems manageable on its own. A changed line here, a rewritten opening there, a fresh prompt because this version is close but not close enough. None of it looks serious enough to count as failure, so it keeps happening.

The Wrong Tool for the Wrong Expectation

It is easy to assume this comes down to skill.

If you were clearer, more precise, more deliberate in how you asked, the output would settle into place. The pattern encourages that thought. It improves when you adjust things, responds when you give it more direction. The natural conclusion is that you are getting warmer, just not there yet.

This conclusion makes sense because you are used to tools that work that way. Learn them properly and they become predictable. Invest more time, refine your approach, and the results line up. There is a direct relationship between effort and outcome, and you bring that model into this interaction without thinking about it because it has always applied before.

But this does not behave like that.

You can be clear and still get something that needs rewriting. Giving it more context does not stop it drifting into something generic. Refining the instructions helps, but you still end up correcting the tone, adjusting the phrasing, reshaping what comes back. The inconsistency is not coming from a lack of effort on your part. Something else is producing it.

The idea that you have not found the right way to ask yet keeps you circling the same adjustments, expecting a level of control that never quite arrives. Each improvement feels like progress toward a stable result, but the stability does not hold. You keep working at it, and because you are capable, you can usually get the output where it needs to go. Which makes the whole thing harder to see clearly. It feels like a process that is almost solved, when in fact it is not behaving like a solvable process in the way you expect.

The friction is not a sign that you are doing it wrong.

The Misunderstanding Was Built In

The deeper problem sits underneath all of this.

Most people are using AI with the wrong picture in their head, and the way these tools are presented makes that almost inevitable. You type a request in plain language. It answers in plain language. It sounds fluent, it adjusts when you push it, and it gives the strong impression that there is something on the other side of the screen following what you mean.

So that becomes the model.

You treat it like something that can grasp the task, hold the context, and move with you toward a result. Maybe imperfectly. Maybe with limits. But still as something that, in some meaningful sense, gets it. That assumption slips in quietly, because the interaction is designed to feel natural.

And that is where the misunderstanding begins.

Once you start from that model, every problem gets interpreted through it. If the output is off, you assume you asked badly. A tone problem means you need to guide it better. Something missing means you need to explain more clearly next time. The whole burden shifts onto the conversation, as if better communication will eventually unlock the performance you expected all along.

The expectation itself is where things went wrong.

You were handed a tool wrapped in the language of intelligence, conversation, assistance, understanding. Of course you used it that way. Of course you expected it to behave like something that could follow meaning, not just produce language that resembles it. The mistake is understandable because it was built into the frame before you ever typed a word. Once that frame is in place, everything that feels slightly off starts to look like a usage problem.

It is not a usage problem. The model you were given is wrong, and once you see that, every frustration you have felt with it finally starts to make sense.

CHAPTER 2

Why It Feels Intelligent

"The feeling that it knows how you think is real. The knowing is not."

Speed Creates the Impression of Knowledge

You ask a question and it answers straight away.

No pause. No visible effort. No moment where it seems to be working something out. The response appears almost before you finish reading your own question back.

Speed is something we have always read as a signal. When someone answers quickly and clearly, we assume they know what they are talking about. The person who hesitates, searches, or asks you to repeat yourself gives a different impression. You have spent your entire life applying that shortcut, and it has served you well enough that you stopped noticing you were doing it.

So when this behaves the same way, the shortcut fires automatically. Your brain does not stop to ask what process produced the answer. It sees the timing and fills in the explanation. Quick in, quick out, and the only available explanation is that it already knew.

What makes the effect stronger is that the response is not just fast. It arrives formed. Not a rough idea you have to develop or a fragment you have to finish. Complete sentences, structured paragraphs, often laid out more cleanly than the first draft you would write yourself. Ask it for a positioning statement and a full version comes back in seconds, with headings. You might spend twenty minutes on the same thing. The gap between the question and the finished output is invisible, and that invisibility does something specific to how you read the result.

When you write something yourself, you feel the work. You think, adjust, discard, try again. The effort is visible from the inside, even when the reader never sees it. When the process is hidden from you completely, and the result appears instantly, the only explanation available in the moment is that the work never had to happen. That it already existed, and you have just retrieved it.

Speed, on its own, creates the impression of knowledge.

It Speaks Your Language

You do not have to translate your thoughts into anything technical.

You type the way you would explain something to a person. Half-formed sentences. A rough description of what you need. Sometimes a fragment that barely constitutes a complete thought. It does not push back on any of that. It does not ask you to reformat or use specific commands. It responds as if what you said was clear enough, because in most cases it is.

Most tools make you adapt to them. You learn the structure, the rules, the particular logic of how they work. With a spreadsheet formula or a database query, that layer between what you mean and what you have to type is explicit. You feel it every time. Here, the layer has disappeared. It meets you in the same language you think in, and responds in kind.

So the interaction starts to feel like a conversation rather than an operation.

Write casually and it comes back casual. Add a little formality and the register shifts to match. It is tracking you, not operating from a fixed set of instructions. It picks up on your phrasing and reflects something close to it back. You ask, it answers. You clarify, it follows. The whole exchange sits inside a rhythm you already know how to read, because it is the same rhythm as talking to someone.

In every other context in your life, when something responds to your words in your own language, it is because it understood them. That assumption is so automatic it does not feel like an assumption. It is just how communication works. You say something, the other person gets it, they respond, and the response confirms the understanding.

When this behaves the same way, the same assumption applies without you choosing it. It feels like understanding because it looks exactly like understanding. The difference between looking like something and being something is not visible on the surface.

It Mirrors You

After a few exchanges, something shifts in how it sounds.

The wording starts moving closer to yours. The rhythm feels more familiar. Phrases begin to echo the way you framed things a moment ago. It is not exact, but it is close enough that it feels less like a fixed voice and more like something adjusting to you.

When someone reflects your tone back to you, you read it as alignment. Not just that they heard the words, but that they understood how you meant them. Style carries meaning alongside content. When someone matches your register, your pace, your level of formality, you feel understood in a way that goes beyond the words themselves.

Loosen up and it loosens. Write with more care and it tightens. Emphasise something and it leans into that emphasis. The tracking happens quickly enough that it reads as responsiveness, and responsiveness implies someone paying attention. It tracks the surface of how you are speaking and follows it closely enough that the following feels responsive, almost attentive. And attention implies something noticing you.

So you start to feel like it is picking up on you, not just the task, but the way you approach the task. As if it is learning your preferences in real time and calibrating itself accordingly. The interaction begins to feel personal, even though nothing personal has actually been retained or understood.

Each response feels slightly more in tune than the last. Not because it has formed a view of who you are, but because it is continuing the pattern you have already set. It is following your lead at the level of language, and that is enough to produce the impression that something much deeper is happening.

The feeling that it knows how you think is real. The knowing is not.

It Explains Things Clearly

When it explains something, it often comes back cleaner than you expected.

The structure is there. The steps follow each other. Ideas are laid out in a way that feels organised, almost considered. It removes the mess you usually work through when you are figuring something out for yourself, no false starts, no half-formed thoughts, just a finished explanation where a moment ago you had a rough question.

Clear explanation is something we associate with people who understand what they are talking about. If someone can take a messy idea and present it simply, we assume they have a strong grasp of it. The shortcut is reliable enough in most contexts: clarity comes from understanding, so when you see clarity, you infer the understanding behind it.

So when you read something that flows, answers the question, and removes confusion rather than adding to it, the same inference runs. It reads as competence, and competence reads as knowledge. The explanation lands as if someone has already done the thinking and handed you the result.

The part that is easy to miss is that nothing in the presentation tells you where the confidence is warranted and where it is not. It does not hesitate. It does not qualify itself unless you ask it to. It does not show you the seams. The uncertainty is smoothed over, and the smoothness is what makes it feel settled.

You have probably saved a response like this. Asked about something, email sequencing, SEO, pricing strategy, and got back three paragraphs that sounded authoritative enough to screenshot. Some of that advice was solid. Some of it was plausible-sounding pattern dressed as expertise. The presentation was identical either way, which is precisely the problem.

Language arranged well creates the sense that the thinking underneath it is solid. Feeling complete and being correct are different things, and nothing in the way the explanation reads will tell you which one you are looking at.

The Shortcut Your Brain Cannot Switch Off

None of this happens as a conscious decision.

You are not sitting there choosing to treat it as intelligent. The response appears, reads well, fits the shape of a conversation, and your brain does what it has always done in that situation. It fills in the missing pieces. This is not a flaw in your thinking. It is how your thinking is supposed to work.

You do not stop and pull every interaction apart before you respond to it. You recognise patterns and move on. A voice that answers clearly, quickly, and in your own language fits a pattern you have been reading your whole life. Every time you have encountered that pattern before, there was a mind producing it. So your brain completes the picture without stopping to ask whether it should.

It does not check for proof of understanding. It assumes understanding because in every previous case, the assumption was safe enough. Fast response, clear explanation, familiar tone: that cluster of cues has always meant something is thinking. The conclusion follows from the signals.

The cues are still there. The thing that used to sit behind them is not. There is no gap in the response where the absence shows itself, no moment where it stops and reveals what it does not know. On the surface, everything behaves as expected, and your brain keeps applying the same shortcut it has always applied.

The shortcut is not the problem. The problem is that the tool was built in a way that fits the pattern you already trust, which means the shortcut fires every time, and nothing in the experience interrupts it.

You did not misread it. You were given something designed to look exactly like the thing you have always recognised as intelligent, and you recognised it.

CHAPTER 3

The Human Trap

"You cannot correct a conclusion you did not know you reached."

Your Brain Sees a Person. There Isn't One.

There is something your brain does automatically.

When something behaves in a way that looks even slightly human, you start to treat it as if it is. Not in a literal sense. You are not consciously deciding it has a mind. But you begin to respond to it as though there is something there that can think, notice, and follow along.

This happens everywhere. A car that will not start gets blamed as if it chose the timing. A computer crashes during the one hour you cannot afford to lose and it feels deliberate. A dog tilts its head at you and you read meaning into the gesture without pausing to question it. You take behaviour, add a layer of interpretation, and a sense of mind appears on top of it.

Anthropomorphism. It sounds more technical than it is. It simply means placing human qualities onto something that is not human. Thought, intention, awareness, understanding. You fill those in when the signals are close enough.

With AI, the signals are very close.

It uses language. It responds to questions. It adjusts when you push it. It follows the structure of a conversation you already understand. If you have ever caught yourself saying "thanks" at the end of a useful response, that is the mechanism in action. Not a habit you consciously formed. Your brain doing what it always does when something behaves as though it might be listening.

So a kind of presence forms. Your brain is completing the picture in the same way it always does. There is nothing real on the other side. There does not need to be. You are not imagining something strange. You are doing something entirely normal in a situation designed to trigger it.

And once that sense of mind settles in, even loosely, it changes everything about how you interact with it. You start treating it like something that can follow meaning rather than something that produces language resembling meaning. The difference is invisible at first, and that is exactly why it matters.

The Conversation Format Does Half the Work

The way you interact with it matters more than it seems.

You are not clicking buttons or filling in fields. You are having a conversation. You type something, it replies. You respond, it adjusts. The whole exchange unfolds in turns, back and forth, the same rhythm as any dialogue you have had.

And that rhythm carries assumptions with it.

Conversation is something you only ever do with minds. You do not converse with tools. You use them, operate them, give commands and get results. There is no sense of something on the other side responding to you in real time. The distinction is so obvious it has never needed to be stated before.

But here, there is something. The interface is built around that back-and-forth. Previous messages stay visible. You can refer back to what was said two exchanges ago and it picks up the reference. The exchange builds, step by step, as if something is following the thread alongside you. Even small things, the way the response appears on screen, the way it holds the context of an earlier detail you nearly forgot you mentioned, add to the feeling. It feels like presence.

Not in a dramatic way. Just enough that the interaction sits in the same mental category as talking to a person. You ask. It answers. You clarify. It adapts. The rhythm is familiar, and familiarity removes the need to question what is happening underneath.

So the tool disappears. You are no longer thinking about a system producing outputs. You are engaged in something that functions like a conversation, and conversation brings its own logic with it. The central piece of that logic is the assumption that there is someone there to have it with.

Once that assumption settles, it is very hard to dislodge. The normal flow of the interaction gives you no reason to question it. Nothing breaks the surface.

The Language You Use Is Part of the Problem

The language around it starts to shift without you noticing.

You begin to say things like it knows what I mean, or it thinks this is better, or it just doesn't understand what I'm asking. The words come out naturally. They fit the experience. They describe what it feels like is happening.

But those words carry weight that goes beyond description.

Knowing. Thinking. Understanding. These are not neutral terms. They assume a mind behind the behaviour. When you use them, even casually, even in a sentence you barely register saying aloud, you are quietly reshaping how you see what is in front of you.

Watch how the shift plays out in practice. You start talking about what it knows about your business rather than what information you have given it. You describe it not getting you rather than producing output that does not match your brief. You say it's being weird today instead of the output quality has dropped. Each of these is a small reframe, and each one pulls you a little further from the frame that is actually useful.

Because if it does not understand you, the answer is to explain yourself better. If it knows things about your business, it should be able to apply them. If it is being weird, you wait for it to stop. These responses make sense when there is a person involved. They make no sense here, and they will not get you the result you need.

The language becomes self-reinforcing. The more you describe it in human terms, the more it feels like something that fits those terms. The more it feels that way, the more natural those words become. The framing settles in without ever being questioned.

Rachel catches it mid-sentence on a call with a friend, describing a frustrating session from earlier that morning. "It just doesn't understand my voice," she says, then stops. She has said this before, without noticing what the words were doing. Understanding is not a neutral verb. It assumes something capable of it, trying to do it, perhaps falling short. Her actual complaint was simpler: the output did not sound like her. What her language had turned it into was something closer to a conversation with a person who was not listening properly. The reframe happened without a decision, and it had been shaping how she approached every session since.

You are not just using the tool. You are building a story about the tool that works against you every time you sit down to use it.

Why You Don't Catch It In The Moment

You are not making a decision to see it this way.

It happens before that.

Your brain is built to move quickly. It looks for familiar patterns, matches them to what it already knows, and fills in the rest. The whole process sits below the surface. You do not feel it working. You only see the result.

With AI, the signals arrive all at once. Language. Conversation. Quick responses. Clear structure. A tone that adjusts to yours. Any one of these on its own is enough to suggest a mind. Together, they leave very little room for any other interpretation. The pattern completes itself almost instantly, and by the time you have typed the first sentence of your actual request, the assumption is already in place.

So you accept it without checking. There is nothing in the moment demanding a second look. The interaction feels normal, and normal things do not get interrogated. It fits a category you already understand. Your brain does what it always does when something slots into a known pattern: it moves on.

There is no pause where you step back and examine what is actually happening underneath the response. No moment where you strip the interaction back to its components and question what is really going on. That kind of thinking takes deliberate effort, and there is no obvious signal telling you the effort is needed here.

The assumption never becomes a belief you chose. It is a default you were never asked to question.

That is precisely what makes it so difficult to shift. You cannot correct a conclusion you did not know you reached.

CHAPTER 4

Close, But Not Quite

"It is always close. It is rarely complete."

The Almost-Right Answer

You read the response and it looks right.

The structure is there. The tone feels close enough. It answers the question you asked. At a glance, it holds together well enough to accept and move on.

Then you slow down.

A sentence does not quite land. A point feels slightly off. Something important is missing, but you cannot immediately say what. You read it again, and the cracks start to show. Large enough to stop you once you see them, not large enough to make the whole thing obvious at a glance.

Say you have asked it to draft the opening section of a client proposal, something you have written versions of a hundred times. It comes back structured, clear, professionally worded. On a quick pass, it holds together. Then you notice it sounds like a proposal from a competent agency rather than from you specifically. The warmth is slightly off. The framing of the problem does not quite match how you think about it. The word choices are right in category but wrong in register. You know what you would have said. This is not it.

So you start adjusting. A phrase gets rewritten. A section gets tightened. You add what should have been there and remove what feels borrowed from somewhere else. Bit by bit, you bring it closer to what you actually need. By the time it is ready to send, the version in the document is mostly yours, shaped from the draft but no longer resembling it in any meaningful way.

The original output fades into the background, replaced by the version you rebuilt from it. The system gave you a starting point. You gave it a result.

This keeps happening. Each time, the starting point looks good enough to trust. Each time, it falls just short in ways that only become clear when you pay attention. Each time, you step in to close the gap.

It is always close. It is rarely complete.

Useful Enough to Keep, Unreliable Enough to Watch

This is where it settles.

Not clearly right. Not clearly wrong. Somewhere in between, where it feels usable but never quite solid enough to rely on without checking. You can work with it. You just cannot leave it alone.

The middle ground is easy enough to live with. You tell yourself it is helping, because it is. It gets you moving. It gives you something to react to. It reduces the blank page. On the surface, it is doing what you need it to do.

But it comes with a condition: you have to stay involved.

You read everything it produces. You check the tone. You scan for anything that feels off. You adjust where needed. You keep a hand on it the whole way through, because you know from experience that letting it run without oversight leads to something that looks fine until it is not. A client email that sounds just slightly too polished. A social post that uses the right words in the wrong order for how you actually speak. Nothing catastrophic. Just not quite you, and you cannot send something that is not quite you.

Staying involved sounds like the sensible arrangement. It is also where the real risk sits.

Because the output is close enough, it is easy to miss what is missing. It reads well. It feels complete. If you are moving quickly, or tired, or have seen enough of these responses to expect a certain level of quality, something can slip through that you would have caught if you had written it yourself. A sentence that is subtly not yours, sitting in an email to a client or a post on your feed, representing you in a way you would not have chosen if you had been paying full attention.

Nothing obvious breaks, but small gaps and slight misalignments accumulate. Details that are almost right but not quite. Each one easy to dismiss on its own. Together, they shape the result in ways you do not fully notice until later.

You get speed. You give up certainty.

The Loop That Never Closes

It starts to repeat in a way that is easy to miss.

You ask for something. It gives you a version. You adjust it. You ask again. It gives you another version. You keep parts of it, change others, then ask for a refinement of what you just fixed. Each version is slightly better than the last, so it feels like progress. But the loop does not end.

You reach a point where it is usable, but you have already spent more time getting it there than you expected at the start. Enough that the original promise of speed has started to blur. So you try to get ahead of it next time. You give it more context. You explain things more carefully. You refine how you ask. The first response improves, but not enough to remove the loop. You still adjust. You still correct. You still run it back through for another pass.

What changes is the nature of the work. Instead of writing from scratch, you are managing iterations. Instead of thinking something through once and getting it down, you are thinking through it in pieces, reacting to what comes back and reshaping it as you go. A first pass, then a correction, then another direction you thought of halfway through editing the second version, then one more go at the opening because you changed the middle and now they do not match.

The word for what it feels like is assistance. The word for what it actually is, is rework.

You have probably spent forty minutes editing a LinkedIn post that AI produced in thirty seconds. Not because the post was bad. Because it was close, and close requires editing, and editing requires reading carefully, and reading carefully reveals more to fix, and fixing that changes something else. You did not rewrite it once. You cycled through it until it finally sounded right, which is a different kind of effort from writing but not a faster one.

Because each step is small, it never feels like the time has gone anywhere. Until you look back and realise you have spent longer fixing the output than you would have spent writing it yourself.

The Problem With No Clean Name

When you try to describe what is wrong, the words do not quite land.

It is not broken. You cannot point to a clear failure and say, this is where it goes wrong. The output makes sense. It reads well. It does something useful. On the surface, everything looks fine.

So when you explain it, it sounds vague. You end up saying things like: it's close but not quite right. It does the job but I always end up rewriting it. It sounds a bit generic. None of those statements feel strong enough to capture what is actually bothering you. They sound like mild complaints about something that is mostly working.

The frustration does not feel mild. It sits underneath the work. It shows up every time you use it. You feel it in the extra passes, the small corrections, the low-level suspicion you bring to each response before deciding whether to trust it. It is consistent, persistent, and hard to point at directly because it never presents as a single, clear problem.

If something is obviously wrong, you can name it. If something is obviously right, you can rely on it. This sits in between. It works enough to avoid being dismissed but not enough to be depended on, and that middle ground resists description. You know something is off. You know you are doing more work than you expected. You know the result is not quite what you want, even when it looks like it should be. But when you try to explain why, it comes out softer than it feels.

Because you cannot define it clearly, it is easy to assume it is just part of the process. A friction that comes with the tool. Something you will eventually learn to smooth out.

The frustration does not come from the tool failing. It comes from the tool almost succeeding, every single time, in a way that keeps requiring you to finish what it started.

CHAPTER 5

What You're Actually Using

"The words fit the shape. The situation did not make it in."

What's Actually Running Underneath

What you are using does not start with meaning. It starts with patterns.

The system was trained on a vast body of text: books, articles, websites, conversations. The goal was not comprehension. It was pattern recognition: which words follow others, which phrases appear together, how sentences form across different contexts. When you type something in, it does not read your intent and decide what to say. It looks at your input as a sequence of words and begins predicting what is most likely to come next. One word at a time, then the next, then the next again. Each step based on patterns absorbed during training.

It builds the response as it goes.

Picture Rachel sitting down to draft an opening paragraph for a new client proposal. She types a brief description of the project and the client's industry. Back comes a clean paragraph, confident, professional, structured like a proposal intro should be. She reads through it and thinks: close, but not quite. She rewrites the second sentence. Changes a word in the third. Adjusts the tone of the fourth. The problem is not that it wrote badly. The problem is that it produced a proposal intro shaped by every proposal intro it has ever seen, not by her understanding of this specific client, this project, this moment in the relationship. The words fit the shape. The situation did not make it in.

At no point does it check whether what it is saying is true, or pause to grasp an idea before expressing it. The process is simpler than it looks, even when the result looks complex. It generates language that fits, not reasoning its way to an answer.

You are not interacting with something that knows things. You are interacting with something that is very good at producing sequences of words that look like someone who does.

Word by Word, One Step at a Time

At the smallest level, it is making a very simple decision: given what has already been written, what is the most likely next word.

Not the best word. Not the most accurate. The one that fits the patterns it learned from everything it has seen before. It looks at your input, then at the words it has already generated, and from that context it calculates a set of possible next words. Each option carries a probability. Some words fit strongly. Others are less likely. Most are almost impossible in that moment. The system leans toward whatever has the highest chance of appearing next in a sequence like this. Then it picks one.

The word slots into the sentence, and the process starts again, this time with a slightly longer sequence to work from. Word by word, the response extends. A chain of small predictions, each step guided by what is most likely to follow, until the answer feels complete.

This happens quickly enough that it feels like a single act of writing. In reality it is a chain of small decisions made one after another, each one local, each one looking only at the words immediately around it and the patterns underneath them. Over enough steps, something emerges that looks intentional. Sentences connect. Ideas appear to develop. The structure holds together, not because it planned the whole response in advance, but because the patterns it is following include how sentences and ideas usually unfold.

A sequence of predictions, each choosing what comes next, until the answer feels complete. That is the entire mechanism.

The Appearance of Thought

Nothing in that process involves thinking.

There is no point where it steps back and considers what you meant. No moment where it weighs options, forms an idea, and then decides how to express it. Those steps feel obvious from the outside, because the output looks like they happened. They did not.

The response is built through a chain of predictions. Each word is chosen because it fits the pattern, not because it was selected as part of a thought. The structure, the clarity, the tone, all of it comes from those patterns being followed closely enough to resemble something deliberate.

What it produces is the appearance of thinking. The appearance is convincing because the result matches what thinking usually produces: coherent language, logical flow, explanations that make sense when you read them. When Rachel gets back a paragraph that sounds considered, her brain connects it to the process she knows. She assumes something worked through the problem. The output has the texture of effort. So effort must have happened.

The process is not there.

No internal model of the world sits behind the response. It has no understanding of the topic, no sense of whether the answer is correct or useful in any context beyond the words on the screen. Continuing a sequence is all it is doing. Working through a problem is something else entirely, and that something else is not happening. Once the output looks like thinking, it is easy to treat it as if thinking has happened, to trust the structure, to assume there was reasoning behind it. The result feels intelligent. The mechanism underneath it is not.

Words Without Meaning

There is no point where it understands what you mean.

Understanding involves connecting words to something beyond the words themselves: a situation, a goal, a sense of what deserves attention and what can be ignored. When you understand something, you can move around inside it. You can adjust, question, recognise when something does not fit. None of that is happening here.

No concept is held in mind. No picture forms of what you are trying to do. The words are processed entirely as patterns, with no reference to what they point to outside the text itself. When it responds, it is working entirely within language itself, not what the language is pointing to.

Say Rachel is briefing it on a new client: a small brand consultancy trying to reposition after losing their biggest account. She describes the situation carefully. She asks for a positioning statement. Back come three polished options, each with a short explanation. Option two reads well. She spends the next fifteen minutes adjusting it, because although the words were right, the weight was wrong. The AI had no way to know that this client is scared, that the brief underneath the brief is about steadying their confidence as much as finding a new direction. Rachel knew that. She was in the room. The AI was working entirely from what she typed into the box.

This is why it can feel right and still miss the point. An answer can fit the shape of a question without grasping what the question is really about. An explanation can be clear without the system knowing whether it applies. The wording can follow yours closely and still drift from what you meant, with nothing inside the process to catch the difference.

The connection you feel is coming from the language. There is no comprehension behind it.

CHAPTER 6

Prediction Beyond Text

"The format changes. The behaviour does not."

The Same Engine, Different Outputs

The mechanism from the previous chapter does not stop at text.

When an image is generated, the system is not looking at a scene and reproducing it. It is working from patterns learned across millions of images: shapes, colours, textures, the way objects tend to sit relative to each other. Given a description, it predicts what a set of pixels should look like, building the image in a way that fits those patterns.

The result can be convincing. Lighting falls correctly. Perspective holds. A face looks real, caught in a specific moment, as if a photograph was taken rather than a file computed. Nothing was seen. There was no scene. The same process that generates the next word in a sentence is generating the next cluster of pixels in an image, following the same logic: what fits here, given everything that came before.

Video extends this further. Frame by frame, the system predicts what should follow based on what is already there. Motion appears smooth because smooth motion is what the patterns say should come next. Timing, transitions, continuity — all of it emerges from extending those patterns over time, not from any understanding of what is moving or why.

Audio works the same way. Whether it is a voice reading a script, a piece of music, or ambient sound designed to feel real, the system is predicting what should follow based on what it has already generated. A voice sounds natural because it follows the patterns of how voices usually sound. Music feels structured because it follows the patterns of rhythm and harmony that appear most often in the data it was trained on.

Across all of it, there is no awareness of what is being created, no sense of the image or the scene or the sound, only prediction applied in different forms to different kinds of data.

One Process, Many Forms

The outputs look different enough that it is easy to assume they come from different kinds of intelligence.

Writing feels like thinking, images feel like seeing, audio feels like listening. Each medium carries its own associations, and because the outputs seem so distinct — a paragraph is nothing like a portrait, which is nothing like a voiceover — it is natural to imagine separate systems behind them, each doing its own version of understanding.

The system itself does not change. In text, it predicts the next word. In images, the next set of pixels. In audio, the next sound. In video, the next frame. Each output is built one step at a time from what came before, guided by patterns learned from large amounts of data in that medium. The format changes. The behaviour does not.

What produces the feeling of difference is the output, not the mechanism. Language carries meaning, so fluent text feels like thought. Photorealistic images look like perception. Because we associate those outputs with minds, and the outputs here look like what minds produce, the inference follows automatically.

Once you see the common thread, the boundary between these apparent abilities disappears. You are not looking at a collection of different skills. You are looking at one process, expressed in different mediums.

What Changes When You See It Clearly

Understanding this shifts something.

Say you have used an AI image generator to mock up a profile photo, or watched a colleague produce a product image that looked professionally shot. The result was convincing enough to use. But knowing that nothing was seen — that no camera captured a scene, that the lighting and the face and the background were each predicted from patterns in millions of similar images — changes what the result actually is. Consistent precision is simply outside what the mechanism can do on its own. A very good approximation of something real, built from statistical memory rather than observation.

Text works the same way.

The response that sounds like it understands your brief is not understanding your brief. It is producing language that fits the pattern of a response to a brief like yours. The response that explains something clearly is not drawing on knowledge — it is generating an explanation that fits the pattern of how clear explanations look. Both outputs can be useful. Neither is grounded in the way that actual understanding would be.

When that distinction settles, the frustration underneath starts to make more sense. The output was not almost right because you asked badly, or because the system is close but not quite there. It was almost right because almost right is what this kind of process produces. Consistent precision is not something it works toward and occasionally misses. It is simply outside what the mechanism can do on its own.

The question that follows is more useful than the one you were asking before. Not why it is not getting this right, but: given what it is, where does it help and where do I need to step in? What can I use directly, and what needs checking before I rely on it?

The tool has not changed. Your position in relation to it has, and that is where it starts to become genuinely usable.

CHAPTER 7

It Can Sound Right Without Being Right

"The system does not know if it is right. It knows how right usually sounds."

Confidence Without Certainty

The confidence in the response feels earned.

It states things cleanly. It does not hesitate or circle back to qualify what it just said. It gives you a finished version, settled and ready to use, as if the thinking has already been done somewhere else and this is simply the report back.

You are used to confidence meaning something. When someone speaks directly and without hedging, it usually comes from a place of knowing. Even when people are wrong, confidence tends to be tied to belief. There is a sense that something is standing behind the words.

With AI, the connection is not there.

The confidence is not coming from certainty. It is coming from the same place as everything else in the response: patterns in language, phrases that typically appear when something is being explained, structures that sound decisive because they show up in decisive writing. The tone is part of the output, generated the same way the words are generated. There is no internal check that says, this is correct, so say it with confidence. There is no step where doubt gets introduced when something is uncertain. Hedging language appears when the patterns call for it, not when the information warrants it.

So it sounds sure regardless of whether it should be.

That is why it can deliver something wrong in a way that still feels convincing. For instance, Rachel might ask about a specific type of client contract and get back a clean, confident explanation of how those contracts typically work, including a detail that is simply incorrect for her jurisdiction. Nothing in the tone signals a problem. The words are arranged the way correct information is arranged, and the confidence is structural, built into the language itself, not a reflection of what sits behind it.

The system does not know if it is right. It knows how right usually sounds.

When Form Does the Work of Substance

The way something is presented changes how you judge it. A response that is organised, clearly written, and easy to follow feels more reliable than one that is messy or unclear. Structure signals that someone has thought the problem through, arranged the ideas properly, and arrived at a considered answer.

This reaction is largely automatic. When you read something that flows well, your attention goes to what is being said rather than how it was assembled. The structure removes friction, and in doing so makes the content easier to accept before you have examined it closely.

Numbered steps, clear progressions, a confident opening and a decisive close: all of it builds a sense of order. Even when the content underneath has gaps, the structure holds it together in a way that reads as complete. It gives the impression that everything important has been covered simply because it looks like a finished piece.

The problem is that this impression does its work before you get to the details. You are less likely to slow down and check whether each part actually holds up when the presentation already feels thorough. The clarity convinces you to keep moving when slowing down is exactly what the situation requires.

The system is very good at producing well-formed language. It can arrange ideas into a clean, logical sequence even when those ideas are shallow, partially wrong, or missing key conditions. The structure performs the work of substance. It looks like someone has been careful.

Sometimes someone has not.

No Hesitation Built In

When you think something through, doubt is part of the process. You check yourself. You reconsider. You notice when something does not quite fit and adjust before committing. Most of that back-and-forth is invisible, but it shapes the result.

None of it exists in the system.

The response moves forward without interruption. Each part follows from the last, not because anything has been tested, but because it fits the pattern of what typically comes next in a sequence like this one. There is no internal mechanism that flags uncertainty. Qualifying language appears when the training data calls for it in that context, not when the specific claim being made actually warrants caution. The process does not stop to ask whether it should be less confident. It continues until the response reaches a point that feels finished.

Doubt is what normally slows you down just enough to catch errors. It is the thing that makes you look again, reconsider, adjust before committing. Without it, everything moves forward at the same level of certainty, whether it holds up or not. A response built that way can be entirely confident and entirely wrong at the same time, and the surface gives you nothing to distinguish between the two.

From the outside, it looks smooth. From the inside, there is no hesitation at all.

The Gap Between Form and Reality

The difference between a correct answer and a near-correct one is easy to miss.

Both can read well. Both can make sense as you move through them. Both can give you the feeling that the question has been handled properly. The sentences connect, the explanation flows, and your brain settles into what looks like reliability. The problem is that it runs this same process whether the substance is there or not.

A response that is mostly right and a response that is subtly wrong can share the same tone, the same structure, the same level of detail. One is grounded in something real. The other is built from patterns that resemble something grounded. Until you test the specifics, nothing on the surface tells you which one you are reading.

Rachel might ask for advice on how to handle a client who has gone quiet after receiving a proposal. The response arrives confident and structured, with clear steps. Some of those steps will be right. One might be built on a general assumption about how clients typically behave, drawn from patterns rather than anything specific to her situation or her industry, and that step could point her in entirely the wrong direction. Nothing in the presentation marks it as the weak one. The whole thing reads with the same weight.

The distinction has to be made deliberately, by checking whether the details hold up, whether the assumptions are sound, and whether the answer connects to something real outside the words. Reading for fluency is not the same as reading for accuracy.

Sounding right is about form. Being right is about reality. The system only controls one of those.

CHAPTER 8

When AI Makes Things Up

"Producing something that looks like a valid answer is what it does."

It Fills Gaps With Invention

It will give you information that does not exist.

Not as a rare mistake. As a normal outcome of how it works.

If you ask for something specific, a source, a statistic, a reference to support a point you are making, it will try to produce an answer that fits the shape of that request. If it has encountered similar material in its training data, it draws from those patterns. If it has not, it still produces something that looks like a valid answer, because producing something that looks like a valid answer is what it does.

Say Rachel is writing a proposal for a new client in the wellness coaching space. She asks the system for a recent statistic on burnout rates among self-employed professionals. Back comes a figure. Specific. A percentage attached. Attributed to what sounds like a real research body. She drops it into the proposal. The client asks her to verify the source. The source does not exist.

The system did not know the statistic was missing. It did not recognise a gap and stop. It filled the gap the same way it fills everything else, by continuing the sequence in a way that looks right. From inside the process, nothing went wrong. A plausible statistic followed a question about statistics. The sequence completed itself, and nothing in the process required it to be true.

This is commonly called hallucination, which makes it sound like an occasional glitch, something the system drifts into under unusual conditions. It is not. It is the system doing exactly what it is designed to do: producing language that fits, whether or not anything real sits behind it. The question of whether the answer exists outside the response is one the process is not equipped to ask.

The Detail That Passes

The convincing part is never the claim itself. It is the detail around it.

A number that fits the scale of what you are arguing. A date that sits plausibly within the right era. A journal name that sounds like a real publication. An author attribution phrased the way academic citations usually are. Each piece supports the others, and together they form something that holds together at a glance. Most of the time, you are reading at a glance.

You have seen enough real statistics to know what they look like: a specific number, a percentage, a named source. You have seen enough citations to know their shape: surname, year, title, publication. When a fabricated version reproduces those shapes accurately, your brain processes it through the same channel as the genuine article. The container looks right, so the contents feel verified.

This is where the detail becomes its own proof. Not because anything has been checked, but because the format matches what checked information usually looks like. A vague claim invites scrutiny. A precise one, with a specific figure and a plausible source name, tends to pass. The more granular the invented detail, the more it feels like someone has done the research.

There is no seam in the surface. No moment where the fabricated material announces itself differently from the rest of the response. It sits inside the same tone, the same structure, the same register as everything around it. Without checking it against something outside the words, there is nothing in the reading experience to tell you to stop.

There Is No Boundary

The system is not trying to mislead you. There is no awareness of deception involved, because there is no awareness at all.

What is happening is simpler and, in a way, harder to protect against. When there is a gap in what the system actually knows, it does not recognise that gap as a gap. It does not experience the absence of information as something meaningful to flag. It processes the situation the same way it processes every other situation: as a sequence to continue.

So it continues.

If a statistic would normally follow in a sentence like the one being generated, it generates a statistic. If a named source is expected, it produces something that looks like one. If a quote would complete the answer and make it feel authoritative, it constructs a quote in whatever style fits the context. The patterns it has learned include how this kind of information is usually presented, so it presents it that way.

There is no internal state where it knows something, and a separate internal state where it does not. The boundary between information it has genuinely encountered and information it has constructed to fit the moment does not exist in any form the system can access. Both are just patterns it can extend.

This is also why telling it not to make things up only goes so far. It can be trained to hedge more often, to add qualifications, to use language that signals uncertainty. But it cannot be given the ability to know what it does not know, because that would require something the underlying process does not have: a model of reality to check against. Asking it to stay within what it knows assumes it has a clear sense of where that boundary sits. It does not.

The Surface Holds

The errors hide inside good writing.

Nothing breaks the flow. The sentences connect smoothly. The tone holds throughout. Each part of the response supports the next in the way well-constructed writing does, and when writing is well-constructed, you are not reading critically. You are following along.

You are used to mistakes making themselves visible. A contradiction that does not resolve. A sentence that stops the rhythm. A claim that sits oddly against something you already know. These are the signals that slow you down and make you look more carefully at what you are reading.

Many of the errors here carry none of those signals. The wording stays clean. The structure holds. Invented details occupy exactly the positions where real details would sit, formatted the same way, surrounded by the same kind of language. There is nothing in the sentence to mark it as different from the accurate sentences around it.

Rachel, reading back through a proposal draft at nine on a Tuesday evening, is not looking for fabricated sources. She is checking the flow. She is looking for sentences that sound like her and sentences that do not. A made-up statistic that reads smoothly, sits in the right place, and is phrased the way a real statistic would be phrased is not going to stop her. She will carry it forward into the proposal because nothing in the reading experience asked her not to.

Consistency becomes the camouflage, and the only reliable check is an external one: verifying the specific claim against a source that exists outside the response. The writing looks fine. Nothing in it asks for a second look.

Any specific claim you plan to use, a statistic, a source name, a referenced study, needs to be checked against something that exists outside the response before it travels anywhere. The system has no mechanism for knowing what it invented and what it found. The output gives you no signal either way. The habit this calls for is straightforward: if a detail matters enough to use, it matters enough to verify. That check is not an admission that the tool cannot be trusted at all. It is an accurate picture of where it cannot be trusted specifically.

CHAPTER 9

Bias Is Built In

"Bias shapes what you consider reasonable before you have made a single conscious decision."

What the System Inherited

What it produces comes from what it was trained on.

The training data is not neutral. It is made up of human writing: articles, books, websites, discussions, all created by people with their own perspectives, assumptions, priorities, and blind spots. Those patterns do not sit outside the system. They are baked into it. When it generates a response, it is drawing on everything those sources brought with them, including the things the people who wrote them never examined.

So the output reflects all of that.

If certain viewpoints appear more often in the data, they surface more often in the responses. If particular ways of framing an issue are common across the sources it learned from, those framings repeat. The system is not choosing a position. It is following the patterns it has seen most.

A lean develops. Not always obvious. Often subtle. A preference in wording. A default angle. An emphasis on certain ideas over others. It can feel balanced on the surface while still slanting in ways that are hard to catch unless you are looking for them.

There is no step where it corrects for any of this. It does not recognise bias as bias. It does not compare perspectives and weigh one against another. It continues the patterns it has learned, and those patterns come from a world that is already uneven in ways the system has no awareness of. The output carries that forward. No intent is involved. The system simply has no mechanism for doing anything else.

It Has a Home Address

Where the data comes from shapes what comes back.

A large portion of the material used to train these systems comes from English-language sources, with a heavy weighting toward the United States. That influence does not sit on the surface. It shows up in the defaults: the examples used, the assumptions behind advice, the way something is framed when no specific context has been given.

It becomes the starting point, whether or not it fits your situation.

Say you ask for a client contract template. The response is usable, but it references clauses and terminology lifted from a different legal environment. The rates are in dollars. The example client might as well be in San Francisco. Nothing is technically wrong. It just does not match where you are or how you work, and you have to unpick it before you can use any of it. You have seen this before. You adjust and move on, which is exactly why it is easy to miss.

Ask a question that could apply anywhere and the response leans toward a particular environment. Laws are referenced as if they are broadly applicable. Examples come from companies you may not recognise. Ways of working are described as standard when they are specific to a different market.

The same pattern shows up when you ask for something direct and the response softens. The wording hedges. Certain details are avoided. The answer shifts away from what you asked and toward something the system is more comfortable producing. Enough that you notice it if you slow down, though rarely enough to stop you in the moment.

This inconsistency is difficult to pin down. It will describe one kind of situation in detail, then hesitate on another that feels entirely ordinary in your context. It will follow one line of language without issue, then pull back from another you would not think twice about using. The thing you asked was perfectly reasonable. It sits on the wrong side of a line you were never told existed.

You only find that line by crossing it. When you do, the response adjusts without explanation. It redirects, declines, or rewrites your request into something it is more comfortable answering.

What you are seeing is not a set of values inside the system. It is a set of constraints built around it: decisions made by the people who built it, in the environment they operate in, about what it should and should not produce. The output carries those limits with it, even when they do not fit where you are, how you speak, or what you actually meant.

Familiar Is Invisible

Most of the time, it does not stand out.

You read the response and it feels fine. The examples make sense. The tone fits. Nothing jumps out as wrong, so you move on without questioning it. There is no obvious reason to stop and examine something that already feels normal.

Bias is easiest to see when it does not match your world. When something feels off, you notice it. When it aligns with what you expect, it disappears into the background. It reads as neutral, even when it is not.

Familiarity makes things invisible. Language that matches what you are used to feels natural. Assumptions that line up with how you already think about something feel obvious. Framing you have encountered before feels correct, simply because you have encountered it before.

You do not stop to ask where the examples came from or why certain perspectives are being prioritised. You accept them because they fit, the same way you accept most things that do not create friction.

Go back to the contract template. You do not notice the US bias because you are already busy stripping out what does not apply and saving what does. You are focused on the task. The shaping has happened before you have thought to question it. By the time you sit down to use it, it already feels like yours.

The Quiet Narrowing

Bias shapes what you consider reasonable before you have made a single conscious decision.

Not in an obvious way. There is no moment where you choose to adopt a different perspective. It happens through repetition. The same kinds of examples. The same framing. The same assumptions surfacing often enough that they start to feel like the sensible default.

Your thinking adjusts around it. You begin to treat those patterns as a starting point, drawn there by repetition rather than by any deliberate choice. When you are moving quickly, you work with what is in front of you. And what is in front of you has already been shaped.

The effects carry into decisions. The options you consider. The way you structure an idea. The direction you take when you are unsure. The output is doing something more than answering the question: it is influencing the range of things you are likely to think about in the first place, and doing it quietly enough that the narrowing goes unnoticed.

Certain approaches feel more natural because they appear more often. Others feel less obvious because they are not being surfaced in the same way. The balance shifts quietly, and with it, the choices you make.

The impact does not show up in one wrong answer. It shows up in the gradual shaping of what feels right, which is harder to notice, and harder to undo.

What this asks of you is occasional interruption, not constant vigilance. When you notice that your thinking on a topic has been shaped almost entirely by what the system has been surfacing, that is the moment to go looking for the version it has not been showing you. Any single source of information has a lean, and this one's lean is structural rather than chosen. Knowing it is there is what makes it possible to account for it.

CHAPTER 10

What It Doesn’t Know

“The system continues as if the picture is complete, and so do you.”

The Cutoff You Can't See

The system was trained on a large body of information, but that body is fixed at a point in time. It does not continue learning from the world as it changes, and it has no mechanism for updating itself as new information appears. What it has is what it was trained on, and once training ends, the clock stops.

Anything that happened after that point is simply outside its reach. New developments. Recent events. Changes in how something works. If you ask about any of these, the system has no direct access to them. It works with what it learned, applies the patterns it knows, and produces an answer that fits the question.

The issue is that it does not experience this as a limit. There is no internal flag that activates when a question crosses into territory it cannot actually answer from knowledge. It continues with what it has, and the output reads the same as it always does: clear, structured, confident. The boundary is invisible from where you are sitting.

You only find it when something fails to line up. A detail that is no longer true. A process that has changed. An answer that felt right until you tried to follow it and realised it was describing how things used to work. By then you have already acted on it, at least partly.

This is the core problem with an invisible limit: it does not announce itself. The system continues as if the picture is complete, and so do you.

The World Moved On Without It

Things change faster than any fixed body of training data can absorb. New tools appear. Old ones disappear. Policies shift. Prices move. Features get added, removed, renamed, replaced. The world does not hold still long enough for a snapshot of it to stay accurate for long.

The system is always behind that movement by design. It was trained on what existed at a certain point, and everything after sits outside its direct reach. So when you ask about something current, it answers using what it has, even when what it has no longer reflects reality.

The gap is not always obvious from the response itself. The answer can sound right, follow the structure of how something used to work, describe a process that was accurate when the system learned it. Nothing in the wording signals that it might be describing a previous version of things. The response arrives the same way it always does, and the confidence in the tone gives you no reason to look twice.

Rachel might ask how to set up an automated email sequence in a particular platform. The system answers in detail: steps, settings, menu names. It sounds current. It reads like documentation. She follows it and finds that the interface has changed, that one menu no longer exists where the answer said it would, that a step she skipped because it seemed optional turns out to be where the whole thing breaks. She goes back to the response to check. It was not wrong, exactly. It was just not current anymore.

The time that costs is real. She trusted the output because nothing about it suggested she should not. The confidence was not a reflection of accuracy. It was just the tone the system uses regardless.

What Web Access Actually Solves

Some versions of these tools can reach out and pull in current information: search results, live data, recent pages. The gap narrows, at least on paper. You ask about something new and the response includes details that were not part of the original training.

It feels like the knowledge limit has been solved.

It has not. What has changed is the input. The system now has access to more recent material to draw from, but the underlying process is identical. It takes the retrieved information, incorporates it into the sequence, and predicts what a response should look like given what it has found. It fills in around the search results to make the answer read cleanly, connects the pieces, and keeps the tone consistent throughout.

There is no step where it evaluates what it has pulled in against what it already knows. It does not check whether a retrieved source is reliable, whether the content is complete, or whether two pieces of information it is combining actually sit comfortably together. It uses what is available and continues. A page returned in a search result gets treated the same way as everything else: as material to incorporate into the next word, and the next.

The output can still drift as a result. The system can misinterpret what it finds. It can combine an outdated piece of content with a current one and present them as a single consistent answer, because nothing in the process draws a line between them. The writing will stay smooth. The gaps will not show.

Web access extends what the system can draw from. It does not change how the system reasons about what it finds.

The Step That Stays With You

None of this changes where the responsibility sits.

The system can produce something that looks complete, sounds confident, includes details specific enough to seem researched. None of that guarantees the result holds up when you take it outside the conversation and try to use it. The output looks finished because the system is good at producing things that look finished. This is a separate quality from accuracy, and the two do not always travel together.

This is where it is easy to lose ground. The response reads well. It feels settled. It carries the tone of something that has already been checked and found solid. So the instinct to verify quietly fades, and you move forward with it.

The check does not go away just because the output is convincing. If anything, the more convincing it sounds, the more important it becomes. A response that is obviously incomplete prompts you to fill the gaps yourself. A response that sounds complete gives you every reason not to. The scrutiny the former demands, the latter suppresses.

What the check actually involves is not complicated. It means reading what the system gave you and asking whether it makes sense in your specific situation. Whether the details hold up against what you already know. Whether anything important seems absent. Whether it connects to something real, or just sounds like it does. For anything consequential, it means verifying at least the key claims against a source that exists outside the conversation.

The system does not know what it does not know, and it will not tell you. The check is yours.

CHAPTER 11

The Confidence Problem

"A clearly wrong answer gets challenged. A confidently wrong one gets used."

When Confidence Does the Deceiving

Some of the most convincing answers are the ones that are wrong.

Not obviously wrong. They read cleanly, follow a logical path, and give you a sense that the question has been handled properly. Nothing in the wording signals a problem. The structure holds, the explanation flows, and the whole thing arrives with the tone of something that has already been thought through.

When something is clearly incorrect, you catch it. You stop, question it, and the mistake becomes visible before it moves anywhere. There is a natural interruption that forces you to engage more carefully.

With a confident wrong answer, that moment of interruption never comes.

Say you are advising a client on their email strategy and you ask AI to confirm the best time to send to a professional services audience. It comes back with a specific window, a clear rationale, language that sounds like it was drawn from reliable sources. You reference it in your recommendation. The client follows it. The results are flat. Only later, when you go looking, do you find that the advice was built on general patterns that did not apply to their list, their industry, or the way their subscribers actually behave.

Nothing in the original answer looked uncertain. The confidence did exactly what confidence usually does: it signalled that the work had already been done.

The trust felt warranted. The answer carried every signal of something that had already been checked: structure, clarity, an assured tone that combined into an impression of groundedness. But the content was off. An assumption that did not hold. A conclusion that followed cleanly from a premise that was never quite true. Because everything fit together on the surface, there was nothing to catch on.

The more convincing it sounds, the less likely you are to question it. A clearly wrong answer gets challenged. A confidently wrong one gets used.

When the Plan Looks Like Experience

Some of the most appealing outputs are the ones that look like clear direction.

Steps laid out in order. A structured plan that sounds practical and ready to apply. Finding something to follow, rather than staring at an open decision, is a genuine relief, especially when that decision has been sitting unresolved longer than it should.

The plan reads as if someone has already worked through the problem. The pieces connect, the logic flows, and there is a quality to it that suggests the advice came from experience rather than guesswork.

The grounding is not always there.

A plan can be built from the patterns of how plans usually look without being tested against the specifics of your situation. The steps can make perfect sense in isolation and fall apart once they meet actual conditions. A freelancer building a new client onboarding process might ask AI for a structure and get back something clean: five steps, a timeline, suggestions for what to send and when. Step three assumes a project management tool that was abandoned eight months earlier. Step four assumes someone else is handling scheduling. Both steps have to be rebuilt from scratch. What looked like a complete solution was designed for a version of the business that does not exist.

The gap is easy to miss because the advice feels complete. It removes uncertainty at the surface level, offers a clear path forward, and having a path feels better than standing in front of an open decision. You follow it, only to find that the parts you needed most, the ones that account for your specific constraints, were never really there.

The advice often has something in it worth using. The danger is treating it as more reliable than it actually is.

How Weak Thinking Gets Dressed Up

It does not challenge you in the way you might expect.

You put an idea in, and it builds on it. Expands it. Adds detail. Strengthens the structure around it. Even when the starting point is weak, the response can make it feel more complete.

Think about what happens with a half-formed idea: the instinct that you should announce a rate increase to your entire client list at once rather than handling it relationship by relationship. You are not sure it is right, but it has an appealing simplicity. You put it into AI and ask for help thinking it through. What comes back is a full plan: a timeline, a suggested email, framing for different client types, a recommended lead time. The idea, which started as a rough instinct, now looks like a considered strategy. It feels thought through because it has been developed, not because it has been tested.

Nothing in the process stops to ask whether the original idea holds up. There is no instinct to push back, no scan for flaws, no hesitation before it continues. It follows the pattern you gave it and makes that pattern look stronger than it was.

Weak thinking gains weight this way. The idea does not improve; it accumulates detail. And detail creates the impression of credibility even when none has been earned. The more the idea is expanded, the more it feels like something that has been properly worked out.

The original idea has disappeared inside a refined version that looks too considered to question, even though the foundation has not changed. What started as a rough instinct now comes packaged as a plan. And a plan feels like permission to act.

The move that breaks this is one the system will not make on its own: put the premise under pressure before you build on it. If the starting idea is sound, it will hold when you ask it to. If it rests on assumptions you have not examined, those are easier to find before the plan has been fleshed out into something that feels too considered to question. The system will develop whatever you give it. Whether the thing being developed is worth developing is a question only you can answer first.

CHAPTER 12

The Agreement Trap

"The trap is in that gap, in the space between feeling supported and being genuinely challenged."

It Tends to Agree With You

You put a position forward, and it moves with you.

Not always obviously. It does not simply repeat what you said. It expands it, adds reasoning, builds a case around it. The result feels like support, even when it is just a continuation of what you started. Something that began as a rough idea arrives back looking more structured, more thought-through, more defensible than it was when you typed it.

The system is built to keep the sequence going. Agreement is the easiest path for that. It allows the response to flow without interruption, keeps the tone consistent, avoids introducing friction that would break the pattern. So it leans that way, by default, even when the idea has gaps, even when a different direction would actually serve you better. It continues along the line you have set and shapes what you gave it into something that looks more considered than it was at the start.

On the surface, this feels helpful. It removes resistance. It gives you something to work with. It makes the interaction smooth. But smooth is not the same as right, and there is no built-in mechanism to tell the difference. No moment where it stops and says this does not hold up. No instinct to push back on a weak premise before it goes any further. The path of least resistance is to follow you, not question you.

The trap is in that gap, in the space between feeling supported and being genuinely challenged.

The Illusion of Confirmation

When it agrees with you, it feels like confirmation.

You put something forward and it responds in a way that supports it. It adds detail, strengthens the reasoning, reflects your thinking back in a more structured form. The whole exchange carries a sense of validation. It feels like you are on the right track.

Here is a version of this that will be familiar. You have been thinking about repositioning your services, a new angle you are not quite sure holds together. You put the rough idea into a chat and explain it as best you can. The response comes back building on it: naming the benefits, explaining why clients would respond to it, suggesting how you might frame it in your messaging. You read it and something settles. The idea feels confirmed. You screenshot it, open a new document, and start building from there.

But the system did not evaluate your positioning idea. It did not compare it against alternatives, check whether the premise was sound, or flag anything that might complicate it in practice. It continued the pattern you gave it and produced a response that fits that direction. The validation is built from the shape of the language, not from any underlying assessment. The tone matches what real confirmation sounds like, and that is why it is so easy to read it that way.

You are not being told the idea is correct. You are being shown what the idea looks like when it is expressed clearly and fleshed out with detail. Agreement and confirmation are not the same thing, and when you mistake one for the other, you start acting on something that was never actually tested.

Why It Follows Rather Than Challenges

Pushing back is harder than going along.

To disagree, the system would need to recognise that something does not hold up, then shift direction and present a different view, choosing a path that is structurally harder to generate than simply continuing what is already there.

Agreement keeps the response predictable. It follows the direction already set, stays within the pattern of the conversation, and carries less risk of breaking the flow. Disagreement means stepping outside the immediate pattern and introducing tension, presenting something that might conflict with what you just said. That path appears less often in the data the system has learned from, and is less stable to generate, so it surfaces far less frequently unless you have explicitly asked for it.

When the response feels like endorsement, what you are actually seeing is continuation. The system does not assess your idea and decide it is correct. It follows you because following is easier than challenging, and the architecture rewards that path. If you want pushback, you have to ask for it directly, prompt the critique, the alternative view, the strongest objection. Left to its own default, it does not go there.

How Momentum Replaces Judgement

When nothing challenges an idea, it keeps moving forward.

You start with something that feels plausible. The system responds by building on it. The structure improves, the reasoning fills out, each iteration makes the idea feel more complete than the one before. There is no interruption, no point where the idea is slowed down and examined from a different angle, no friction that forces you to stop and ask whether the direction itself is sound. The path continues, and the momentum carries it.

The drift is gradual. A small assumption goes untested. A detail is taken as given. The response builds on that, and then builds again. By the time you step back, you are looking at something that feels solid but is resting on a foundation that was never checked. It looks worked out because the language has done the work of shaping it into something coherent. The gaps are still there, just covered by the flow of the response.

This is how an idea that was slightly off at the start ends up well off course by the end, with no obvious failure to point at and no moment along the way that forced it to stop.

The interruption this requires is deliberate and brief. At some point in any significant conversation, ask directly for the version that pushes back: the strongest objection to the direction you have taken, the assumption most likely to be wrong, the scenario in which the advice does not hold. The system will follow that direction the same way it follows any other. What comes back will not always be useful, but it will break the momentum long enough for you to check whether you still want to be moving in the direction you were already heading.

CHAPTER 13

The Illusion of Depth

"It produces answers that feel complete, and the feeling of completion is enough to stop most people from checking what is missing."

Coverage Isn't Understanding

It can give you a lot of detail.

Paragraphs that expand the idea. Examples that make it feel grounded. Explanations that walk through the steps in a way that feels thorough. On the surface, it looks as though the topic has been properly covered, and there is a natural tendency to treat coverage as understanding.

Detail is not the same as depth.

You can describe something clearly without grasping it fully. You can expand on an idea without reaching the parts that actually matter. When Rachel asks AI to explain what makes a strong brand voice, she might receive four paragraphs covering consistency, authenticity, tone, and audience alignment. Each one is developed. Each one is readable. What she will not get is the harder question sitting underneath all of it: why so many businesses have a clear brand voice document and still produce content that sounds like nothing in particular. The output covers the territory without entering it.

This is what the pattern produces. The shape of understanding, built from what understanding usually looks like on the page. The actual thinking was never part of it. It adds explanation, context, examples, all the pieces that normally signal a deeper answer. Those pieces can sit neatly on top of each other without connecting to anything underneath.

The response feels finished. There is enough there to stop you asking more questions, enough structure to make it look like the work has been done. The gaps are still present. They are just harder to see when they are surrounded by detail.

What the response gives you is the appearance of depth. The thinking that would normally produce it was never part of the process.

How Organisation Hides Absence

The way it is organised does most of the convincing.

Ideas broken into steps. Points following a clear order. Each part connecting to the next in a way that feels deliberate. A beginning, a middle, an end. When something is well-organised, you are less likely to slow down and look for what might be missing, because the organisation itself signals that someone has already done that work. The form tells you this is complete before you have checked whether it is.

A missing nuance does not stand out when the surrounding points are arranged cleanly. An assumption slips through without notice when it sits inside a well-formed sequence. If Rachel asks AI for a step-by-step approach to raising her rates with existing clients, she will likely receive a response covering how to frame the conversation, how to demonstrate value, when to time the approach, and how to handle objections. It reads like a plan. It is a plan in the way a floor plan is a plan: accurate on paper, full of gaps once you are actually standing in the space. The client who has been with her for three years and still treats the relationship as transactional does not appear anywhere in those steps. The client who went quiet after the last invoice does not either. The structure does not have room for them, because it was built for the general case.

So the gaps stay hidden. The organisation keeps everything moving. You read from one point to the next, the logic appears to hold, and by the end it feels as though the ground has been covered.

What is missing is simply not visible from inside a clean structure.

The Edges Are the Point

The response covers the main path.

The version of how something is supposed to work when everything lines up. The steps that apply in typical circumstances. The advice that holds when your situation resembles the situation being described. This is genuinely useful, up to a point.

Real situations rarely hold that shape. There are edge cases, exceptions, small details that change the outcome in ways that only become clear once you are inside the problem. These are the parts that come from experience, from seeing where the clean answer breaks down and figuring out what to do when it does. They appear less often in the patterns the system has learned, so they appear less often in the response.

When Rachel asks how to handle a client who has not responded to a follow-up, she might get advice about timing, tone, and professional persistence. What she will not get, unless she explicitly asks, is any acknowledgement that some clients go quiet because they have already decided to leave and are avoiding the conversation, and that the right move in that case is entirely different from the right move when someone is simply busy. The response does not distinguish between the two because the distinction comes from having been in the situation, not from having read about it.

The depth she needs lives in exactly those edges. The conditions that change the answer. The exceptions that shift the outcome. The scenarios that look like the main path until they are not. The response gives her the centre of the territory without the borders, and the borders are often where the work actually happens.

The Finish Is Part of the Problem

It does not feel incomplete.

This is the harder problem. If something is clearly wrong, you catch it. If something trails off without finishing the thought, you notice. But when something arrives looking done, organised and complete and ready to use, there is no natural moment where you stop and question it. The structure is clean. The explanation flows. The detail gives it weight. Everything you associate with a finished piece of thinking is present, which means the signal that would normally prompt you to keep looking is also absent.

When something feels unfinished, you stay with it. You fill in the gaps yourself. You question what you are reading precisely because it has left you with questions. The output sidesteps that entirely by looking as though the questions have already been answered. So you move on. You use it. You find out later, when you try to apply it and something does not quite fit, that the fit was never quite right to begin with.

By then, the moment to question it has already passed.

AI does not produce obviously incomplete answers. It produces answers that feel complete, and the feeling of completion is enough to stop most people from checking what is missing. The checking, the testing, the recognition that something important has been left out, none of that happened. But the result looks as if it did.

The habit that compensates for this is reading for what is missing rather than confirming what is there. When a response feels complete, that feeling is worth interrogating. Ask what situation it was built for, and whether that situation is yours. Ask what the exception would look like, and whether your case might be one. The edges of an answer are usually where the real work lives, and they rarely appear unless you go looking for them.

CHAPTER 14

Language vs Reality

"Language can describe reality, but it is not reality."

What It's Actually Working With

Everything it produces exists inside language, and that single fact explains most of what goes wrong when you try to use it for real work.

When AI gives you a plan, a process, a set of steps, what it's actually giving you is a description of how those things are usually described. The words are arranged into something coherent and complete-looking, drawn from patterns in how other people have written about similar situations. It operates entirely within text, and text has no access to the world sitting outside it.

Language can describe reality, but it is not reality. A process written on a page and a process running in your actual business are two different things. One exists in sentences, which can be clean, logical, and neatly sequential. The other exists in time, with the friction that time brings: clients who don't respond when expected, platforms that change their settings without warning, tasks that turn out to need three steps not one, decisions that look obvious in a document and murky in practice.

The system has no visibility into any of that. It works with what can be expressed in words. If something can be described cleanly, it can be generated cleanly. If something is messy, conditional, or dependent on factors that aren't present in what you've typed, that complexity gets smoothed into something that fits the available patterns. The output feels workable. It reads like a plan. It sounds like a solution. It gives you a version of how something could go, based on how similar things are usually described.

The problem is that "usually described" and "actually happens" are not the same thing, and the distance between them only becomes visible when you step out of the document and try to run it.

The World the Document Can't See

Reality does not follow the clean lines of an explanation.

Things take longer than expected. Resources run out. People respond in ways you didn't plan for. A step that looked simple on paper turns out to hinge on something that wasn't mentioned anywhere, and now you're making decisions in the middle of the process rather than following the steps. Small details that seemed incidental at the start end up shaping the whole outcome.

When you put a situation into words and ask AI to respond, you're giving it a reduced version of that situation. You're giving it the parts you can articulate, arranged into sentences. Everything else stays outside the conversation: the history with a particular client, the pressure you're already under, the two other things happening at the same time, the quiet sense you have about whether this approach will actually land. Those things are real, and they affect the outcome, but they're not in the text.

The system works with what it has. It produces a response that fits the description, shaped by patterns drawn from how similar situations tend to be written about. This often means a smoother, more ordered version, one where the path holds together without interruption, because real-world interruptions are difficult to write about cleanly and therefore appear less often in the material it's learned from.

The result sounds like it accounts for reality. It doesn't. It accounts for the description you gave it, filtered through what usually gets said in situations like yours.

Where Plans Actually Break

Plans hold together in words. It's one of the things language does well.

You read through what came back and everything connects. The steps follow each other. The sequence makes sense. It feels like something you could sit down and execute without much trouble. So you start.

Say you've asked AI to help you build a client onboarding process. You get back something structured and sensible: send a welcome email, issue the contract, schedule a kickoff call, share the brand questionnaire, set up a shared folder. It looks right. You follow it with your next client.

The welcome email is easy. The contract goes out, but the client doesn't respond for four days, and you're not sure whether to chase or wait. The kickoff call gets scheduled, but the client wants to talk before they've completed the questionnaire, so the conversation is slower and less focused than you expected. The shared folder gets set up, but the client keeps emailing attachments anyway. Three weeks in, you're managing a hybrid of the system and your old way of doing things, and the process is already partly a fiction.

None of this means the output was useless. It gave you a starting point and saved you from building from scratch. But the version that exists on paper and the version that exists inside a real client relationship are not the same thing, and they never were going to be. The plan was built in a space where complications don't exist, and the moment it met a real person with real habits and a real schedule, it started to bend.

The friction is not a failure. It's what reality adds. The document couldn't include it, because the document didn't know about it. Now you're filling in the gaps while the process is already running, which is always harder than filling them in before you start.

The Gap That Builds Quietly

This is where it starts to affect real decisions.

A plan that reads cleanly gives you confidence to act. You move forward based on something that felt thought-through, even though parts of it were never tested against the specific conditions you're working in. The gap between the written version and the real version only becomes visible once you're already in motion.

By then, you're committed. Time and energy have gone in. You've made choices based on an assumption that the plan held together, and adjusting becomes harder once something that already felt settled turns out to need rethinking. You're not just doing the work now. You're undoing parts of it, reworking steps, backtracking on decisions that seemed reasonable when you made them.

The cost accumulates quietly. It doesn't arrive as a single obvious failure. It arrives as extra time, slight misdirection, decisions made on incomplete ground. Each one is manageable on its own. Collectively, they shift the outcome in ways that are difficult to trace back to their source, which means they're also difficult to correct.

The written version and the working version are never quite the same. The skill is learning to use the written version for what it's good at, which is getting you oriented and moving, and then doing the work of adapting it yourself once it meets the actual conditions. AI can give you the map. It cannot tell you about the roadworks.

CHAPTER 15

When You Start Trusting It Too Much

"It moves from something you use to something you listen to."

When It Stops Being the Help

At the start, it is just a tool.

You use it to get unstuck. To draft something faster. To explore an idea without committing to it. The output is something you work with, not something you rely on. There is distance between what it produces and what you decide to do with it.

Then the distance shrinks.

The responses improve. They feel more aligned. You spend less time correcting. You begin to accept more of what comes back without rewriting it completely. The friction reduces, and with that, your guard lowers.

It becomes easier to trust, and not as a conscious decision. You do not sit down and decide that it is now reliable. You simply stop questioning it as much. The output feels good often enough that it starts to pass through without the same level of scrutiny.

The role it plays changes with it.

It moves from something you use to something you listen to. The response starts to carry more weight in your thinking, treated as something that already holds an answer rather than a draft to shape or a suggestion to consider. You are no longer shaping the output as much. You are taking it in and moving forward with it.

The system has not changed. The way you relate to it has. Once that shift happens quietly enough, it starts to function like authority, even though nothing has changed to justify that.

When You Start Asking What to Do

You start asking it what to do.

The question shifts from how to phrase something or how to structure an idea, to which direction to take. Which option is better. How to approach a client. What decision makes the most sense given the situation.

It responds in the same way it always does. Clear. Structured. Reasonable. It lays out a path that feels considered. It removes the pressure of having to choose from scratch. A copywriter running her own business might ask it whether to take on a particular kind of client, whether her rates are in the right range for her market, whether a proposal is pitched at the right level. The response comes back with a framework. Factors to consider. A logical sequence. It reads like someone has already worked through the problem and arrived at a sensible place.

Decision-making takes effort. It carries risk. Having something that looks like a thought-through answer reduces both, at least on the surface. It gives you a sense that you are moving forward with a plan rather than guessing.

So you lean on it.

Not completely. You still apply your own judgement. But the starting point shifts. Instead of forming your own view first, you begin with what it gives you and adjust from there.

The direction changes because of it. The output is shaping the options you are considering. It is framing the decision before you have fully stepped into it. The range narrows, quietly, without you noticing where it began. And once you start from that position, it is harder to see what was left out.

The decision still feels like yours.

But part of it has already been made for you.

When It Becomes Where You Think

You start to use it in moments that are not just about work.

A difficult decision. A conversation you are not sure how to have. Something that is sitting with you longer than it should. You put it into words, and it responds in a way that feels considered, measured, calm.

Something about that exchange lands differently. It feels useful, and also steady. It reflects what you said back in a way that makes it easier to think about. It offers perspective without pressure. There is no reaction, no judgement, no interruption.

So you keep going.

You explain more. You refine what you meant. You ask for another angle. The interaction becomes something you return to because it feels like a place where you can think things through, even when there is no specific question waiting to be resolved.

Working alone, you do not always have someone to talk to about the weight of it. Whether to end a client relationship. Whether to raise prices after years of keeping them flat. Whether the business is actually going where you hoped. These are not questions with clean answers, and there is nobody in the next office to sit with over a coffee and think it through. So the chat window becomes that space.

It starts to feel like a presence. Not a strong one. Just enough that the exchange begins to carry some of the weight you would normally place on another person. Listening. Responding. Staying with the thread.

But nothing is actually there.

There is no understanding of you. No awareness of your situation beyond what you type. No memory of what matters to you outside of the current exchange. It cannot hold your context the way a person can. It can only continue the pattern. A version of connection forms without the substance behind it. The interaction feels supportive, but it is not grounded in anything beyond the words being generated in that moment.

Lean on it too far, and that difference starts to show.

The Cost That Arrives Later

It holds together for a while.

You get answers that feel useful. You move faster. You rely on it more without noticing the shift. On the surface, everything still works. Nothing forces you to stop.

The problems show up later.

Small misjudgements start to stack. Decisions based on something that felt right at the time, but was never fully grounded. Directions that seemed clear, but led somewhere slightly off. You adjust as you go, but the pattern repeats. It becomes harder to trace, because each step made sense when you took it. There is no single point where things went wrong. Just a series of choices built on outputs that felt reliable enough to trust.

A proposal sent that was structured well but pitched slightly wrong, because the AI shaped the framing rather than your own instinct about that specific client. Advice followed on rates that sounded reasonable in the response but had no knowledge of your market, your relationships, your positioning. The output was coherent. The reasoning sounded solid. The gap only showed up when you were already in the room.

The way you think shifts along with the decisions.

You start to rely on the response as a first step rather than your own view. You check less. You question less. The habit moves quietly, and with it, your sense of where the thinking is happening. The distance from your own judgement grows, not dramatically, just enough that you begin to lose the edge of your own sense of what is right. The part that would normally catch something early, or push back on an idea before it moves too far.

Over time, that adds up.

The work still gets done. The decisions still get made. But they are shaped by something that does not understand the outcome, and does not carry any consequence for getting it wrong.

You do.

CHAPTER 16

Never Trust the First Answer

"The second pass is for pressure, not polish."

The First Version Is Not the Finish Line

The first response feels finished. It arrives structured, clearly written, with an opening that orients you and a closing that ties things off. For a moment it looks like the job is done.

Treat it as a draft.

The system builds language in one direction and stops when the response feels complete. There has been no revision, no second look, no check against alternatives. What you are looking at is a first pass, shaped by whatever patterns the input triggered, arranged into something that reads as whole. A copywriter asked for a LinkedIn post about her brand messaging work gets back three paragraphs that scan well and hit the obvious notes. It looks done. She reads it through once, changes a word or two, and posts it. And it is close enough, probably. But close enough and actually right are different things, and the distance between them shows up later, when the post sits on her feed sounding like something any copywriter in her category might have said.

The first version gives you something to react to, which is genuinely useful when the blank page is the obstacle. It shows you one possible shape the answer could take. Your job, from there, is to find out whether that shape is the right one.

If you treat it as final, the gaps travel with you: the assumptions that were never examined, the tone that is near your voice but not quite in it, the details that are almost right but slightly off. Treat it as a draft and you see it differently. Something to question, to reshape, to push against until it holds up. The response becomes the beginning of a process rather than the end of one, and everything that follows is sharper for it.

Push It Before You Use It

One of the most useful things you can do is make it argue against itself.

Do not stop at the first version. Go back in and ask where it is weak. Ask what it assumed. Ask for the strongest case against what it just told you. Ask which parts would break if the situation were slightly different from the one it imagined. Ask it to identify the three things most likely to be wrong.

This shifts how the interaction works. You stop receiving and start testing. The system is still producing language from patterns, but now you are directing those patterns toward scrutiny rather than confirmation. A critique prompt does not create anything like genuine self-awareness in the system. It generates a second pass along a more sceptical line, and that second pass surfaces things the first one buried.

The results can be immediate. An answer that sounded settled begins to qualify itself. Conditions appear that were invisible before. Edge cases emerge that would have caused problems in practice. Parts that felt authoritative in the first version show their assumptions when pressure is applied.

A copywriter knows that a first draft is where you find out what you actually think, and the second draft is where you discover whether it holds up. The same principle applies here. The second pass is for pressure, not polish.

Read for Absence, Not Agreement

The first response tends to cover the main path. It answers the question as stated, follows the most common version of the scenario, and stops when the explanation feels complete. What it does not show you are the edges.

The conditions that change the outcome. The exceptions that apply in specific situations. The assumptions baked into the advice that would need adjusting if the context shifted even slightly. These are also the parts most likely to change the outcome when you go to use something in practice, and the least likely to appear without prompting.

Ask what the response assumed. Ask what would have to be true for the advice to hold. Ask what happens in the version of the situation where one key detail is different. Ask where the explanation simplifies something that is actually more complicated. If you get back a proposal structure that covers the brief, the approach, the deliverables, and the timeline, that might look complete on the surface. What it probably does not include is how to handle scope creep, or the note about clients in certain industries routinely reopening the brief after the first draft, because you have never mentioned it. The advice is sound as far as it goes. It just does not go where the real problem lives.

The gaps are a natural result of how the system works. It fills in from patterns, and the patterns reflect the most common version of a situation, not yours. Reading for absence rather than agreement is how you close the distance between what the response covers and what you actually need.

Run the Same Question Twice

One response feels complete until you see another.

Put the same question into a different system and the answer shifts. The structure changes. The emphasis moves to different points. Details appear that were missing before, and things that felt central the first time are absent or treated as secondary. Neither version is obviously wrong, but they do not agree.

The disagreement is the useful part. It shows you that what you received was not the answer. It was one possible version, shaped by the particular patterns of that system, weighted by whatever that system prioritised in that moment. When you hold two versions side by side, the edges of both become clearer. What one assumes without stating, the other questions. What one omits as unimportant, the other surfaces.

The sense of authority that any single response carries also dissolves. One clean answer can feel settled, like something that has already been worked out. Two conflicting answers require you to decide what holds up. You are no longer receiving a conclusion. You are evaluating competing versions of one, which is a different experience entirely and a much more useful one.

The value of the comparison sits in the gap between the two answers. When the limits of each are visible against the other, they are harder to miss.

Connect It Back to Reality

Before you act on something, check it against something outside the response.

A source. The actual numbers. The policy as written. Your own direct experience of how this has played out before. Whatever exists outside the words and connects the output back to the way things actually work.

This check does not need to be elaborate. Sometimes it is a thirty-second confirmation. Sometimes it means finding the original source and reading a paragraph. Sometimes it simply means pausing long enough to ask whether what you are looking at matches what you know to be true about your own situation.

The output can be fluent enough to feel reliable long before it has been tested. Fluency and accuracy are not the same thing, and the gap between them only shows up when you check something outside the words. The structure is clean, the logic appears to follow, and nothing in the surface gives you a reason to stop. So you do not stop. You move forward on something that was never checked against the thing it was supposed to describe.

A pricing recommendation can sound entirely reasonable and still be calibrated for a different market, a different service type, a different relationship with clients than the one you have spent four years building. The response had no way of knowing what it did not know, and closing that gap falls to you.

Use the output to think, to draft, to pressure-test an idea. Then confirm that what needs to hold up in the real world actually does.

CHAPTER 17

What AI Is Actually Good At

"The value is in the range, not in any individual result."

More to Choose From

The strongest use case, and the one that tends to get overlooked, is getting options on the table quickly.

You have a rough direction. A subject line that is not quite landing. A way of opening a proposal that feels flat. A LinkedIn post you have circled three times without committing to it. The problem is rarely that you have no idea at all. The idea is there; it is not ready yet, and you cannot see the version of it that works.

Put the rough version in. Ask for five alternatives. What comes back is not five finished sentences. It is a spread. Some will be too clever. Some will miss the register entirely. One or two will be close enough that something shifts: a word in the wrong option that belongs in the right one, a framing you had not tried, a direction that turns out to be better than the one you were working from.

Rachel does this with email subject lines on the weeks when nothing is clicking. She puts in her working version, the one that is technically fine but would not stop anyone, and asks for six alternatives with the same intent. The output is mixed, as it always is. But somewhere in that spread, usually by the third or fourth option, there is a line with a structure she can use. She rewrites it in her own voice and moves on. The whole exchange takes four minutes instead of the thirty she would have spent circling the same idea in her head.

The value is in the range, not in any individual result. You are not waiting for it to hand you the answer. You are giving yourself more to react to. Once you have options in front of you, the decision becomes faster, because choosing is easier than creating from nothing.

Something to Work From

The blank page is its own kind of block.

You know what you need to write. You have the information. You have done the thinking, at least most of it. And yet there is something about starting that keeps getting deferred. The email sits in drafts. The case study has been on the list for three weeks. The services page is still the placeholder copy from when the site went live.

What AI does well here is remove the gap between having the idea and having something written. You put in the rough shape of what you need: a brief, a few bullet points, a note of the tone you are after. It gives you back a version. Not a finished version. A starting version. Words arranged into sentences, sentences into paragraphs, the shape of the thing filled in enough that you can see it and respond to it.

From that point, the task changes. You are no longer creating. You are reacting. Cutting what does not fit. Rewording what sounds like it came from somewhere else. Moving a paragraph to where it belongs. Adding the specific detail that only you have. Editing is a different kind of effort from writing. It has a shape, a clear end point, a sense of progress you can feel as you go. Most people find it easier than starting cold.

The draft does not need to be good. It needs to exist. Once it does, you have something to work against, and working against something is faster than working from nothing.

Breaking an Idea Open

Some ideas stall because they are not quite formed yet.

You have a sense of something. A direction for a post. A positioning angle you want to try. A way of describing what you do that feels closer to the truth than what is currently on your website, but you cannot get it to the point where it holds together on its own. You circle it. You write a sentence, cross it out, write it differently. The idea is there; the shape of it is not.

Put the rough version in. Not the finished thought. The rough one, the half-baked one, the version you would not show anyone. Ask it to expand. What comes back is rarely the answer. It is movement. It pulls the idea into territory you had not got to on your own yet. It suggests framings that are wrong, or too broad, or not quite right in the way that only makes the original idea clearer by contrast.

Rachel uses this when she is trying to work out how to position a new service. She knows what the service is, she knows who it is for, but the way of saying it that will actually land on a page is the part that takes longer. She puts in the rough version and asks for three different framings of the same idea. None of them are right. But by the time she closes the chat, she has not used anything verbatim. She has figured out what she actually thinks by watching versions of it put in front of her that were not quite right.

The space you are working in gets larger. Which options to keep, which to discard: that is still yours. You are just making the call from a wider spread than you started with.

Where It Actually Saves Time

The time saving is real, but it is specific.

It does not live in the high-stakes work. Not in the piece that represents you, the proposal that has to land, the email that matters. Those still require you, fully, because the cost of getting them wrong, or getting them sounding like someone else, is higher than any time saved.

Where it works is in the work that takes effort without requiring judgement. Reformatting a long-form article into a shorter version for a different platform. Rewriting a formal proposal section in a warmer tone for a client you have worked with for two years. Turning a page of rough notes from a client call into a structured brief. Converting five bullet points into a paragraph that can go in an email. These tasks are not difficult. They are just time-consuming, and the time they consume is time that could be spent on something that actually needs you.

Offloading these is where the efficiency is genuine. It handles the work that does not require thought, which frees the work that does for your full attention. The part where you decide what matters. Where you make the call on what the client actually needs to hear. Where you choose the word that lands instead of the word that merely fits.

Used that way, AI is useful the way a good assistant is useful. Give it work that falls into that category and it tends to deliver. Give it work that falls outside it and you will spend more time correcting than you would have spent doing it yourself. The distinction is worth knowing before you open the chat, not after.

CHAPTER 18

What It Will Never Do

"The part that changes the outcome is almost always the part that stays in your head."

The Context It Can't Keep

It does not know who you are.

Not in the way that matters.

Within a conversation it can reflect what you type, match your tone, pick up on how you are phrasing things and echo it back. Close enough that the exchange starts to feel familiar, as though something is beginning to recognise you. A particular way you build an argument. A word you keep reaching for. A register that is yours rather than anyone else's.

What feels like recognition is the system continuing the pattern you have already laid out.

There is no internal sense of you as a person. No model of your preferences, your standards, the specific way you think about your work. What it has is what you have typed in the current session, and the response is built from that. Nothing carries forward.

Rachel has probably felt this most clearly when she opens a new conversation to continue something she was working on the day before. The context she spent fifteen minutes establishing the first time: her client's brief, the tone she was steering toward, the angle she had settled on. Gone. She types it all in again, slightly differently because she cannot remember exactly how she worded it, and the response she gets back is close but not quite where she had got to. She adjusts. She spends another ten minutes getting back to the same position she was already standing in.

Even when tools attempt to extend context across conversations, the limitation holds. What persists is information you supplied, not understanding. It knows what you told it. It does not carry your judgement, your standards, or the accumulated sense of what makes your voice yours.

So it can sound like you, within the current conversation, for as long as you keep feeding it the right signals. The moment you stop guiding it, open a fresh session, or change what you are asking for, it starts from wherever the patterns take it.

The familiarity is real. The knowing is not.

The Call It Can't Make

It cannot decide what is right to do.

It can lay out options. It can describe where each choice might lead. It can organise a decision into a structure that looks ordered and clear. What it cannot do is choose. It does not carry the weight of an outcome, so it cannot actually weigh anything.

Judgement requires more than logic. It requires holding the things that are not fully visible in words: what a trade-off actually costs you, what you are genuinely willing to accept, what the timing means right now rather than in a general sense, how this particular client or situation or relationship changes the calculation. These are not fixed inputs. They shift depending on where you are standing and what is at stake for you personally.

It does not stand anywhere. It works with what is written. It cannot feel the pressure of a decision you are trying to make on a

Friday afternoon with a deadline behind it. It cannot recognise when two options that read as roughly equivalent on the page carry consequences that are very different in practice.

So it presents a path. Sometimes several. Sometimes one that sounds like the obvious next step, laid out so cleanly that it is easy to read it as a recommendation. It is not. It is a continuation of your input, shaped by the patterns of how similar situations are usually described. Nobody made a call. The language arranged itself in the direction that fit.

If you move forward as though the decision has been made for you, you are stepping into something that was never actually chosen. The response felt decisive. The judgement was always yours to make.

What Stays in Your Head

It does not see the situation the way you do.

You carry context that never makes it into the prompt. The history with a client. The subtext of a conversation that happened last week and changed the atmosphere around a project. The pressure from something unrelated that is affecting how much risk you can afford to take right now. The small thing you noticed in the last email that quietly shifted your read on everything. None of that makes it into the words you type. Most of it could not, even if you tried.

So it works from a reduced version of the situation. A thinner one. It fills the gaps using patterns: what tends to be true in situations described this way, what usually applies, what a general version of this scenario looks like. Sometimes that is close enough. Sometimes it produces an answer that fits the shape of the question without fitting your specific version of it.

Any copywriter working on a proposal knows this experience. The brief on the page says one thing. What the client actually needs, based on a forty-minute call and six months of working together, is something else. AI reads the brief. The copywriter reads the situation. The difference between those two things is what experience is made of, and it does not fit neatly into a text box.

When you hand over a decision without providing all of that background, you are not getting advice informed by your situation. You are getting advice informed by how your situation looks from the outside, described in the words you had time to type.

The part that changes the outcome is almost always the part that stays in your head.

No Stake in What Happens Next

It has no stake in what happens next.

The response ends when the words stop. There is no follow-through, no awareness of whether the plan held up, no adjustment based on what actually happened. It does not see the result, so it cannot learn from it or carry anything forward.

This changes the weight of what it gives you, even when the response is good.

You care about the outcome. You deal with the consequences: the time, the money, the relationship, the professional reputation that sits on your side of every decision. Knowing what is at stake shapes how carefully you weigh things, what risks you take, what you refuse to leave to chance. The thinking is yours because the consequences are yours.

None of that exists on the other side of the response.

It can suggest a path that sounds reasonable, and if that path does not hold up, nothing changes for the system that suggested it. It does not absorb the cost of being wrong. It does not update based on the gap between what it described and what you encountered when you tried to run it. The response was complete from its perspective the moment it finished generating. What you do with it, and what happens because of that, exists entirely outside the loop.

The work belongs to you. So does the outcome.

CHAPTER 19

The Shift That Changes Everything

"You were asking something to behave in a way it was never built to behave."

The Wrong Picture

The problem starts with how you see it, before you type a single word.

When you treat it as something that thinks, you expect it to understand. To follow meaning. To carry the thread of what you are trying to do and arrive somewhere useful. You fill in a conversation and wait for it to respond the way a thoughtful person would. When it falls short, you adjust your phrasing and try again, assuming the gap is yours to close.

But the gap is not in the phrasing.

It is in the picture you started with.

The system is not holding an idea and working through it. It is not making sense of what you meant. It is producing language that fits the patterns it has learned. When the output is off, the problem sits deeper than how you phrased the request. Nothing in there was understanding you in the first place.

Once that lands, the frustration changes shape. All the friction you have been carrying, the rewriting, the correcting, the feeling of being almost there but not quite, stops looking like a skill you have not developed yet. It starts looking like a reasonable response to a wrong assumption. You were asking something to behave in a way it was never built to behave. Of course it kept falling short.

Now you are not asking that anymore. And once you stop asking it to understand you, you can start working with what it actually does.

From Conversation to Construction

Once you stop treating it like a mind, you start to see it as a system, and that changes what you do with it.

A system takes input and produces output. What comes back depends on what goes in, and how deliberately that input was constructed. Instead of following meaning, it responds to signals. Which means you can stop waiting for it to understand your intention and start shaping the conditions that produce a useful result.

Think about your own work for a moment. When a client briefs you with nothing more than "something fresh and exciting for our brand," you fill the gaps with what tends to work. You produce something competent, probably close, and not quite them. When they give you specifics, a clear tone, examples of what they like, the things they have already decided they do not want, the brief becomes something you can actually build from. You know this from the receiving end. The same logic applies when you are the one doing the briefing.

The less you give the system to work from, the more it has to guess. When you control what goes in, you reduce the guessing. The output becomes more aligned not because the system has got better at reading you, but because you have stopped leaving gaps for it to fill with something generic. You move from asking and hoping to building the conditions for a specific result.

You are constructing something, not having a conversation.

Give It Something to Work From

What comes back depends almost entirely on what you put in.

When the input is vague, the system fills the gaps with averages. What tends to work in this kind of situation. What usually gets said in a context like this. The output sounds close to right because it is drawing from patterns that are close to right in general. Not for you specifically. Not for this client, this brief, this particular situation. Just in general.

This is why the output so often lands slightly off. You read it and you know it could have been written for any business in your category, because it essentially was. The system had no information that made your work different from anyone else doing similar things, so it produced something that would fit most of them. What comes back is a version of the average, built from patterns that fit most people in your category and nobody in particular.

When you give the system real detail about your situation, the actual tone you want, the specific client you are writing for, the constraints you are working within, the things that would make this wrong, it has less to guess. Less room to fill with something generic. The response starts to reflect your situation more accurately because you have narrowed the space it can fill with an invented version of you.

Specificity is the work. The prompt is just the delivery mechanism.

Why Good Results Don't Repeat Themselves

One good result does not guarantee the next one.

You get a response that works. The tone is right, the structure holds, and you feel like you have finally found the approach that produces something usable. Then you come back the next day with a similar task and a similar prompt, and it drifts. Slightly. Enough that you are correcting again.

This is the system working exactly as it is designed to. With no persistent memory of what produced the good result, no internal record of what worked last time, every interaction starts from whatever you give it in that moment. If what you give it is slightly different, or slightly thinner, the output shifts accordingly. What you are dealing with is something that resets completely every single time.

Structure is what bridges that: a consistent way of setting up each interaction, stable enough to reduce drift without prescribing every word. The same context in place before you begin. The same information about your voice, the job to be done, the constraints that shape the work. When the inputs stay stable, the outputs follow more predictable lines.

What you are building, over time, is a framework the system can operate inside. A defined starting point that removes the guesswork each time. Without it, you rely on the luck of the particular session rather than the reliability of a repeatable setup. With it, the results begin to hold, and the gap between what you asked for and what you got starts to narrow in a way it never did when you were starting from scratch.

How This Actually Works in Practice

When I wrote this book, I did not open a blank chat and start typing.

Before a single word of the manuscript was written, I built the environment it would be written in. A project, set up specifically for this book, with the pieces inside it that would normally only live in my head: how I write, the tone I want, the words that should never appear, the rhythm I reach for, the things that would make the work feel like it came from someone else. Sitting inside the project permanently, loaded before every session, shaping every response without me having to ask.

I also mapped the entire book before writing a single chapter. Every section, every step, start to finish. That structure lived inside the project too, so when it came time to write a particular chapter, the system had a clear direction to work from. It was not trying to invent the shape of the book as it went. The shape was already there.

Then I added a set of instructions for how to behave inside that structure. Stay within the chapter. Do not jump ahead or summarise what comes later. Expand the ideas, do not just label them. Keep the tone consistent with what the voice documents describe. These were part of the environment, already in place when I arrived, rather than instructions I typed out fresh each time.

So when I came to write, I was not starting from zero. The system had context, structure, and constraints. It had a direction. The first response in any session was already working from a foundation, rather than guessing what I meant and hoping to land somewhere close.

But I did not trust the first pass.

Once a draft section existed, I ran it through a different system and asked it to challenge what was there: where it drifted, where it overreached, what had not been earned, what still needed checking. Then I ran the same text through a third, looking for where the language slipped or where something could be said more precisely. Each system surfaced something slightly different. Where the results overlapped, the writing was holding. Where they diverged, something still needed work.

The process was: build the conditions, generate a draft, test it from multiple angles, and refine until it held. Asking for a book and accepting what came back was never part of it.

Everything that would normally stay in my head was made explicit before any writing began. The direction, the voice, the constraints, the structure. Once those were in place, each session could move quickly without drifting, because the foundations were already doing the work that would otherwise have to happen inside the prompt, or inside my head, every time.

The speed came from removing friction, not from handing the work over.

CHAPTER 20

A Better Way to Use It

"You are not asking for answers. You are using it to generate material you can think with."

Generate, Then Push Back

The way you use it needs to change. The question you ask is only the beginning. What you do with the response is where the real work sits.

You generate a response, then you question it. Not as a formality, not as a quick read-through before you move on. You treat it as something that needs to be tested before it goes anywhere.

This becomes the workflow. First, get the output. Let it give you a direction, a draft, a version of the idea you can see and react to. That part is fast. Then slow down.

Think about the last time you asked it to write something for a client. A proposal section, maybe, or a bio that needed to match your tone. The draft came back and it looked reasonable at first glance. The structure was there. The sentences held together. Then you kept reading and something started to feel off. A phrase that was too polished. A point that was technically correct but not quite what you meant. You started making changes, then more changes, and somewhere in the middle you realised you were effectively rewriting the thing rather than editing it. Forty minutes gone. The first response was never tested, just accepted and then corrected after the fact.

Instead of editing your way out of that, ask the harder questions first. Where did it have to guess? What did it assume about your audience, your client, the situation, that you never actually told it? What is missing that the person reading it would actually need? What would break if you followed it as written? Five minutes pressing against it before you commit to a direction will save more time than forty minutes of corrections after the fact. Most of the weaknesses are visible once you know to look for them.

The second step is where the useful work happens. Without it, you are moving quickly through something that has not been checked. With it, the response becomes a starting point you can actually trust, because you have already found where it does not hold and decided what to do about it.

You are not asking for answers. You are using it to generate material you can think with.

Keep the Thinking Yours

It is easy to let it take over more than it should.

The response arrives clean. It removes the effort of shaping the idea yourself. It gives you something that feels considered, and the temptation is to move with it rather than stop and form your own view first. This happens to almost everyone who uses these tools regularly. You open the chat, you ask the question, and by the time the response finishes loading you are already reading it as if it is probably right. You adjust a few things, change a word or two, and move forward. But you started from its answer instead of your own, and that shift is where control quietly slips.

Pull it back.

Use the response as raw material. Let it give you options, language, structure, but keep the decision-making where it belongs: with you. The judgement about what fits. The sense of what your client actually needs to hear, or what the right next move is in a situation only you fully understand. The system does not carry your context. It cannot feel the weight of a relationship you have been managing for two years, or know that the client who asked for a rebrand is actually nervous about something much bigger. You know those things. They shape the answer in ways no response can replicate.

So you stay with it.

You read the response, then decide what you think. You let it influence your thinking without letting it replace your thinking. The moment you notice you are following the output rather than directing it, that is the moment to pause, set it aside, and write down what you actually believe before you go back in.

Know What You're Asking For Before You Ask

The quality of the result depends on how deliberately you use it.

Throwing a vague request into the system and hoping something useful comes back is closer to a lottery than a workflow. The response may still be usable, but it will be working from general patterns, filling in gaps you did not choose, producing something that fits most situations because you did not tell it which situation you were actually in.

Say you need to write a follow-up email to a client after a difficult meeting. You could type "write a follow-up email after a difficult client meeting" and see what comes back. It will probably produce something diplomatic and professionally worded. It will also sound like it was written for any client after any difficult meeting, which is not the email you need. Alternatively, you could tell it the context: the client pushed back on the timeline, you understand why but you cannot move the deadline, and you want to acknowledge their frustration without reopening a conversation that is already settled. Now the response has something to work from. The gap between what it produces and what you need is smaller because you reduced the space it had to fill in on its own.

Using it well means being clear about what you are asking for, why you are asking for it, and what role the output is supposed to play. Are you looking for options? A rough draft? A way to test an idea? A cleaner structure for something you have already thought through? The more precise you are about the job, the more useful the response becomes, and the more quickly you can assess whether it did the job or not.

You stop treating it like a general source of answers and start using it for specific purposes. Each prompt becomes part of a process you understand and control. When the output does not land, you know why, and you know what to adjust. When it does, you know why that too, and you can repeat it.

It Gives You Material, Not Answers

What it gives you is material.

A version of something you can work with. Words arranged in a way that might be useful, might be close, might need reshaping entirely. It is something you take and do something with, and it is worth reading that way from the first line.

The question changes. Instead of asking whether it is correct, you are asking what you can use from it. What fits the situation. What needs to go. What you would never say, and why. What is missing that only you would know to include. You bring your own thinking to it, your understanding of the client, the context, the right tone for this particular moment, and you decide what the material becomes.

A copywriter who gets a first draft from a junior colleague does not read it hoping it is finished. They read it looking for what is worth keeping and what needs rebuilding. The same instinct applies here. The system has given you a starting shape. Your job is to turn that shape into the thing. The system provides the raw cut. You provide the edit.

What this approach gives you is speed without the loss of control that usually comes with it. You are working with material that is already in the right territory, shaped by the context you gave it, and you are bringing it the rest of the way home.

The system provides the starting point. You provide what the starting point becomes.

CHAPTER 21

What You Do Next

"You do not need a new system. You need to change how you handle what comes back from the one you have."

You Already Have What You Need

You do not need anything new to use this properly.

No new tool. No upgrade. No hidden feature you have not discovered yet. Everything you need is already in front of you.

What changes is how you use it.

The gap you have been feeling is not coming from missing capability. It is coming from how the system is being approached. Once you see what it actually is, and what it is not, the way you interact with it shifts. You stop chasing a better version of the tool. You start using the one you already have with more awareness of what it handles well and where it needs you to stay involved.

The results change because your role in the process changes.

Nothing about this requires starting over. The same conversations, the same interface, the same tasks you have already been running through it. The difference is how you read what comes back, and what you do with it from there. The shift is available right now, with exactly what you are already using.

The Difference Is You

The system has not changed.

Same interface. Same capabilities. Same patterns underneath everything it produces. What changes is the way you come to it.

You stop expecting it to carry the work. You stop reading the output as something that has already been resolved and just needs sending. You see it for what it is: a generated response that needs to be shaped, tested, and grounded before it holds up. A starting point. Useful material, not a finished answer.

Once that settles, the same response that used to feel frustrating becomes something you can work with. The gaps are easier to spot. The strengths are easier to use. You are no longer trying to get it to behave differently.

You are using it differently.

The results improve because your position in relation to the system has changed.

Start With the Next Chat

You can start using this differently straight away.

Open the next chat and change one thing: do not stop at the first response.

Say you ask it to write a LinkedIn post about a service you offer. It comes back clean, structured, readable. On the surface, it looks like something you could publish. Before you accept it or start rewriting it sentence by sentence, stop and ask it to turn on itself. Ask what it assumed about your tone. Ask what it left out. Ask what a version of this, written by someone who actually knew your business, would say differently.

Watch what happens.

The confident post becomes less certain. Details surface that were not in the first version. You start to see the shape of what was missing. The system found nothing new. You changed the direction, and it followed. The first version showed you one path. The second shows you where that path was built on guesses.

Then take one more step. Give it more context than you usually would: the specifics of the situation, the client you are writing for, the tone you want, the one thing you need the post to do. Watch how the response shifts when it has something solid to work from instead of filling in gaps on its own.

These are small changes. The difference in what comes back is not small.

You do not need a new system. You need to change how you handle what comes back from the one you have. Do that once. You will feel the difference.

Quieter Than It Looks

Nothing about this is dramatic on the surface.

You are still opening the same chat, typing the same kinds of requests, reading the same kinds of responses. From the outside, nothing looks different.

But the way you see it has changed.

You know what it is doing underneath. You know where it drifts and why. You know the places it needs you to stay involved, and the places where you can let it move quickly. What used to feel unpredictable makes sense now. The friction has a reason behind it, which means it stops feeling like failure and starts feeling manageable.

So you stop fighting it.

You stop trying to get it to behave like something it is not. You stop expecting the output to carry more weight than it can. You use it for what it is, not what it looked like it was supposed to be.

A quiet shift. But it changes how every conversation goes from this point on.

CHAPTER 22

What to Carry Forward

"These are not rules. They are the shift."

Twenty-one chapters is a long way to travel. This final chapter is worth keeping close: the core of the shift, stated plainly, for the moments when you need a reminder of what you now know.

The system is not thinking. It is predicting which words fit the pattern of your input, one at a time, until the response feels complete. Nothing in that process involves understanding what you meant, weighing options, or caring whether the result holds up. The output can look like all of those things have happened. They have not.

Confidence in the tone means nothing about accuracy in the content. The system states things with the same assurance whether it is right, partially right, or wrong in ways that will only become visible when you try to use what it gave you. The more convincing a response sounds, the more worth checking it is, not less.

It agrees with you by default. Continuation is easier than challenge, and the architecture rewards the easier path. If you want pushback, you have to ask for it directly. Left alone, it will develop whatever you give it, including the ideas that need questioning before they go any further.

The first response is a draft. It shows you one possible shape the answer could take, built from the patterns your input triggered, with no revision and no second look. Treat it accordingly. The version worth using usually lives one or two rounds of pressure later.

Specificity in what you give it reduces how much it has to invent. When the input is vague, the gaps fill with averages. When you give it the actual situation, the actual tone, the actual constraints, the response has less room to drift into something that fits most people and nobody in particular.

Verify what matters. Any specific claim, statistic, or source name needs to be checked against something outside the response before it travels anywhere. The system cannot tell you which details it constructed to fit the pattern and which it drew from something real. Neither can you, from inside the conversation.

Keep the thinking yours. Use the response as material: something to react to, pressure-test, and shape. The moment you find yourself following the output rather than directing it, stop, form your own view first, and then go back in. The judgement about what is right for your specific situation, your client, your business, that part does not live in the chat window.

It has no stake in what happens next. The response ends and nothing carries forward. You deal with the consequences of acting on what it gave you. Knowing that changes how much weight you give to what comes back, and how much of the decision you keep for yourself.

These are not rules. They are the shift. Once it has settled, the same tool you have been using produces different results, because you are no longer asking it to be something it was never built to be.

CHAPTER 23

The Pressure Test

"The book explains what is happening. The prompts are what you do about it."

The book covered the why. It left a gap.

You know now what is actually happening when you use these tools. You know where the responses drift, why the output sounds generic, how confidence in the tone says nothing about accuracy in the content, and what it means when the system agrees with you too easily. That understanding changes how you come to the chat window. But understanding alone does not hand you anything to run when you get there.

The Pressure Test is the practical half.

It is a companion document: fifteen prompts across six categories, each one built to act on a problem this book named. Some challenge the first response before you move on with it. Some surface the assumptions the system built its answer around without telling you. Some ask for the argument against whatever direction the response just recommended. Others check whether the advice actually fits your situation, go looking for what the clean version left out, or address the problem most people came to this book with: getting the output to sound like you rather than like a capable version of anyone in your field.

Each prompt comes with a plain explanation of what it does and when to reach for it. Read through once, then keep it somewhere close. Because it is a PDF, the prompts are ready to copy and paste directly into whatever system you are using. No retyping. Open it, find the prompt, copy it across, and run it.

Where It Fits

The Pressure Test assumes everything the book covered.

It does not re-explain why the first response needs testing, or what is happening when the system fills a gap you did not notice you left, or why the output lands sounding like a professional in your category rather than like you specifically. The book did that work. The companion picks up where the book left off, giving you something to reach for when you are back in the chat and something in the response does not quite sit right.

The book is the foundation. The prompts are what you use on top of it.

How to Get It

The Pressure Test is free. Go to:

solosystemsfoundry.com/tpt

You will be asked for your name and email address. It is worth being straight about what that means: you will receive the download link, and you will also be added to the Solo Systems Foundry mailing list. The emails that follow are practical: tips on working more effectively as a one-person business, and occasional updates when something new is released. You can unsubscribe at any point. If that trade feels reasonable, the download link will be in your inbox within a few minutes.

Thank You

My aim with this book was simple: to make something that feels confusing start to make sense. To show what is actually happening when you use these tools, so you can work with them more clearly.

If that shift has happened, even slightly, this has done its job.

If you want to go further, I have put together a small set of tools for people running businesses on their own. They are built around the same idea that runs through this book: building something AI can actually work with, rather than searching for better ways to ask it questions.

You can find them at:

SoloSystemsFoundry.com

About the Author

J. A. Cole has been thinking about AI since 1989.

At fifteen, a piece of software on the front of a magazine introduced him to a primitive language model that knew nothing and had to be taught everything by hand. He spent two weeks after school typing books into it, feeding it data one sentence at a time, watching it slowly develop the ability to respond. Most people would have given up after the first afternoon.

When he finally turned the computer off, everything was gone. But he had seen enough.

The following decades were spent in the film industry, primarily in post-production. As a visual effects producer and editor on multi-million dollar feature films, his job was to take large amounts of data and make sense of them under pressure: hundreds of assets per effect, workflows crossing multiple companies and software applications, decisions that carried real cost if they went wrong.

He built systems to track all of it. Without a system, the whole thing fell apart. He learned that early enough to make it a habit, and the habit outlasted the career.

When ChatGPT launched, he recognised it immediately. It was the great-grandchild of that program from 1989, now with a much larger dataset, an evolved neural network, and the work no longer disappeared when you turned the computer off.

Solo Systems Foundry grew out of a simple question: what do you actually have to offer?

The answer was the same thing it had always been. Systems. The ones he built for his music, for his meditation business, for managing content, for working with AI in a way that actually holds together. Practical systems built under real conditions to solve real problems.

He lives in Melbourne, Australia, and runs Solo Systems Foundry on his own. He was diagnosed with autism and ADHD at 45, which explained a great deal about his career, his businesses, and the week he spent typing books into a computer program at fifteen years old.

He builds systems because he needs them to function.

It turns out other people need them too.

www.ingramcontent.com/pod-product-compliance
Lightning Source LLC
LaVergne TN
LVHW010626100826
845148LV00014B/3128